P9-CEK-313

A CONCISE HISTORY OF Ireland

A CONCISE HISTORY OF

Ireland

MÁIRE AND
CONOR CRUISE O'BRIEN

with 174 illustrations

BEEKMAN HOUSE · NEW YORK

Frontispiece. Detail of carved
monk and knight, from the
cloister of Jerpoint Abbey. Late
12th century. *Photo Commissioners of Public Works in Ireland.*

CONTENTS

CHAPTER I

Prehistory, Myth and the Earliest Records

Prehistory in Ireland is an impersonal affair until you come to the great stone tombs. These – although we can date their beginnings as long ago as 3000 BC – present a challenge to our contemporary understanding in terms that we feel constantly on the verge of re-solving. What is more, we know that from the time of our earliest records, at the beginning of the Christian era, Irishmen have been similarly preoccupied by them. Before them we can reconstruct only a rudimentary pattern of human life on the island, going back to the point when – in the Middle Stone Age – the fishermen and food-gatherers of post-glacial Europe, following the coastlines and the forest edges, crossed from Scotland into Antrim to find and exploit the flint deposits there. They may have come dry-shod, before the disappearance of the land-bridges, but more probably they navi-gated the narrow strait in skin coracles. No prior traces of man's habitation can be shown to survive; the Early Stone Age hunter does not seem to have come so far. Probably because of this the remains of the giant deer we call the Irish Elk abound.

The giant Irish elk – six feet at the shoulder, eight feet across the antlers

The Mesolithic people are believed to have been our earliest ancestors, a continuing and considerable basic element in our physical stock and the originators of some of the characteristic practices of our intensely conservative country life – the coracle was still in use within living memory on the Bann and the Boyne. Being fisher folk, these ancestors loved the water-side, lake and island, and this preference conditioned the siting of homesteads for some thousands of years afterwards. Later comers reinforced these dwel-ling-sites against changing lake levels, and later again, in the metal-using ages, we find men building and occupying artificial islands, called *crannóg* in Irish, some of which were still lived in in the seventeenth century. Nevertheless, our common humanity apart, we can tell very little about Middle Stone Age man; we cannot guess his beliefs; we do not know how he disposed of his dead. All this changes with the New Stone Age.

The Neolithic inhabitants of Ireland were farmers; they cultivated the soil and raised domestic animals. They possessed a formidable repertory of skills and materials. Their sophisticated stone axes were mass-produced in factories and traded far afield. For their houses, defences, boats, weirs and causeways they consumed enormous quantities of timber. They had mastered the techniques of pottery, spinning and weaving. They cooked their food and ground their corn for bread – the saddle-quern they used was still employed in Ireland in the Middle Ages. They occupied the hill-tops above the heavier low-lying soils, bog and woodland, difficult of tillage, and, in their time, the entire island of Ireland was populated.

From their time also we date the first appearance in Ireland of people who built in massive stone, not dwelling-places but sanctuaries, burial-places for their dead and perhaps temples for their gods. Literally thousands of these remain: chambered mounds and cairns, free-standing dolmens, stone circles and alignments, and solitary standing stones. We call them 'megalithic', meaning 'built of great stones'. We can distinguish two distinct and probably independent traditions, both of which we can trace back to the Mediterranean. Immeasurably the most impressive of these stone sanctuaries are the decorated passage-graves.

These are very often grouped in cemeteries and advantageously sited to command attention – the most celebrated one crowns the ridges along the bend of the Boyne – and there is some evidence of

The great standing stone at Punchestown, known as the Long Stone

The Long Cairn of Creevy-keel (*opposite*), the Poulnabrone Dolmen (*left*), and the great tumulus of Dowth (*below*), are but three among Ireland's thousands of megalithic monuments

solar orientation. Immense labour and much social organization must have been needed to erect them. The ornamentation on the carved stones, executed entirely without metal tools, is grave, exuberant, expert and controlled, but the disposition of the decorated stones in kerb and walling appears to us arbitrary. If there is a pattern we cannot apprehend it. Can we detect the stylized human figure? Would the carvings on the upright stones seen by inconstant torchlight simulate draperies? Was the content of the symbols forgotten and only the conviction of their sacredness retained? We cannot answer these questions. What is certain is that, when we are first able to disengage the mythology of pre-Christian Ireland from the euhemerization – that method of interpretation which regards myths as traditional accounts of real incidents in history – of post-Christian learning, the great city of tombs on the Boyne, *Brú na Bóinne*, is specifically the abode of the gods, the burial-place of kings and a centre of superstitious awe. Other sites had similar associations; Tara is the outstanding example.

The first antiquaries of Ireland, writing between the Scandinavian raids and the Norman conquest, envisaged her early history as a

This decorated stone basin is in the passage-grave of Knowth (*right*), where more carved decoration is seen on the massive upright stones. Whorls and spirals on megalithic monuments were executed without metal tools

series of invasions going back before the Flood. These accounts are highly stylized and often patently fictitious, so that a modern reaction has been to dismiss the entire schema. Furthermore, the basic pattern of an agricultural and pastoral society which we find established for prehistoric Ireland is so essentially conservative that many authorities are reluctant to invoke hypotheses of conquest to account for innovations. They prefer to attribute these to peaceful commercial interchange. Nevertheless, much of the traditional material, though unhistorical in any strict sense, reflects startlingly – as we shall see later on – situations we know to have existed. It must be remembered that an incursion of the type that might give rise to a folk-memory or impose a burial-cult in circumstances of sparse populations having relatively low defensive capabilities need not involve any great numbers. A tribal offshoot, a small specialized war-band, could constitute itself an aristocracy without greatly disturbing the substructure over which it established ascendancy. It seems impossible to account for the emergence of Iron Age Ireland, in significant part Celtic-speaking, and certainly conquest-minded, on any other terms.

The Hill of Tara, Co. Meath, seat of half-legendary kings and a centre of superstitious awe; traditionally associated with the 'High Kingship', it was an important burial site in prehistoric times

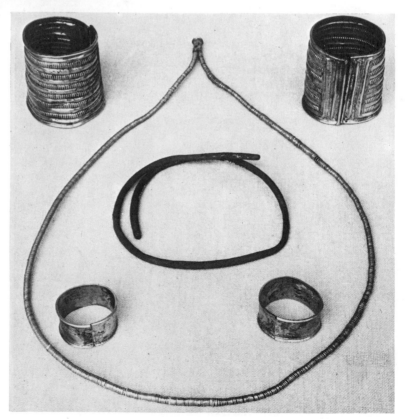

The Celtic Bronze Age produced many outstanding examples of craftsmanship in armour, weapons and articles of personal use and ornament. *Top*, bronze goad decorated with birds; *above*, decorated bronze shield; *right*, Bronze Age gold hoard, including bracelets and necklets

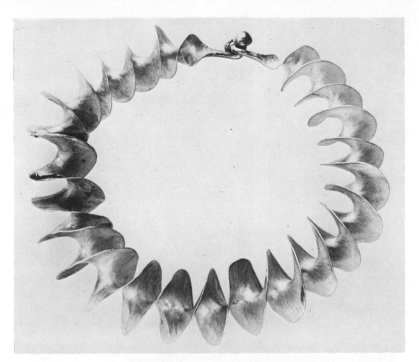

Twisted gold torc, or collar,
of the Late Iron Age

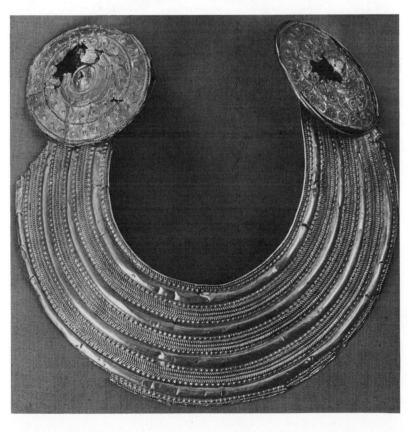

Gold lunula (neck‑plate) of
the Early Bronze Age

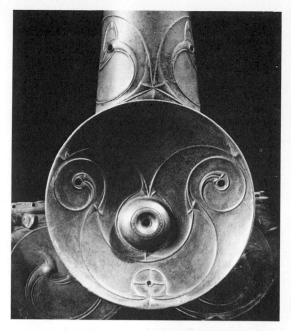

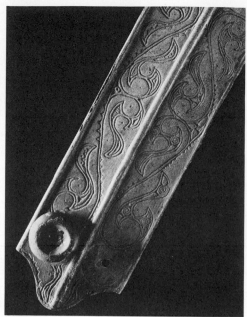

The Petrie Crown: pagan tomb ornament or Christian votive crown? It exemplifies the late continuance of La Tène motifs in Irish insular art (*above, left*). The similarly decorated bronze scabbard (*above, right*) is considerably older

The Turoe Stone, in Co. Galway, is covered with typical La Tène – Late Iron Age – decoration. It is just under four feet high, and suggests a phallic cult

The Bronze Age in Ireland lasted fifteen hundred years, and left us a brilliant and diversified craftsmanship to admire: weapons of bronze – the beautifully balanced leaf-shaped sword – and exquisitely distinctive personal ornaments of native gold. The new metals were versatile, but scarce and costly, and many Stone Age methods and materials continue unsubmerged. The people left no records, but we know they were aware of the solemn nature of the great tombs; on occasion they buried their dead within their enclosure. They may have continued the cult of mighty stones; many of our 'ceremonial' stone circles are attributed to them. As the end of their era begins to run parallel to recorded history their aesthetic impulse stagnates; the ornaments are more massive, the motifs stereotyped. The first elements of the Iron Age herald an almost total change of style.

The Iron Age as we know it in Ireland is not the Iron Age of *The Celts* Rome. It traces its descent from the movement across Europe from east to west of the barbarian iron-using peoples whose cultural evolution and territorial displacement can be traced back seven hundred years before the Roman invasion of Britain – in archaeological terms from the cultures of Hallstatt and La Tène – from the *Keltoi/Celtae* of the classical world, the sackers of Rome and of Delphi. The evidence points to a complex of self-contained tribal units among whom warfare, internecine and external, was endemic. Enough fragments of their speech survive to show that we are concerned with that branch of the development of the Indo-Germanic languages which we term 'Celtic' – although we do not know that the speakers ever referred to themselves or thought of themselves as Celts.

What we know of their religion, customs and practices reinforces our sense of a common culture whose salient features correspond strikingly to those presented by the body of Irish tradition. Where they moved and settled, their gods moved with them, gods who can be identified from place, tribal and personal names, whose own names and attributes are recorded in European history and engraved on European monuments, whose doings are encapsulated in Irish and Welsh literature. The social organization is that revealed by the Irish laws even down to the ramifications of the complex system of clientship and surety which cemented the structure of kin and tribe, of king, nobles and free commoners. Their learned and priestly orders, Caesar's druids, retained their prestige in Ireland, long after the coming of Christianity, as poets and 'judges'. The seating at their feasts, their word for beer, the importance of the 'champion's portion', their ritual boasting, their lime-dressed hair, their head-hunting, their chariot-fighting, their single combats, their going

15

The Broighter gold torc

naked into battle, their sacrifices and divination, even their cast of mind – their liking for allusive and hyperbolic speech, their fond, ness for the triad – are matters of record in classical texts, while each particular trait can be paralleled from Irish sources.

Finally, in an Iron Age hoard unearthed at Broighter in Co. Derry we find a gold collar, or torc, with La Tène ornament of the kind that can be seen in wear on the statues of Celtic warriors commemorating the victories of Greece and Rome. Some time between its manufacture and the coming of Christianity, if not be, fore, Ireland became a Celtic-speaking country.

There is no doubt that the general pattern of successive small-scale incursions and conquests by culturally and linguistically related, but politically independent, tribes is the key to the reality of what took place. Each tribe had a pantheon and origin-legends proper to itself, yet all derived from a basic common theology. Just such a divine assemblage, gone underground, emerges in the stories of Finn, and we recall the heroic oath of Cuchulain, hero of the Ulster epic, the *Táin Bó Cuailnge* or 'Cattle-drive of Cooley'; 'I swear by the gods my people swear by!' Conquerors of this type feel compelled to placate the divinities they displace, most especially the goddess of the soil beneath them which may otherwise withhold its fruits; hence the persistent convention of the 'marriage' of Irish kings with the sovereignty, conceived as a goddess.

The names by which Ireland and the sister island were known to the Mediterranean in the world of the seventh century BC are still re, cognizable today: Ierne – Latin Hibernia – is Ireland; Albion, once the whole island of Britain, is now retrenched to Scotland. On Ptolemy's map dating from the second century AD a surprisingly high number of places and peoples can be identified: the Pretannic Islands, for example, readily as the British Isles. These are in Irish the islands of the *Cruithni*, named for a group of tribes in, habiting both, and including the historic Picts. The contrast of

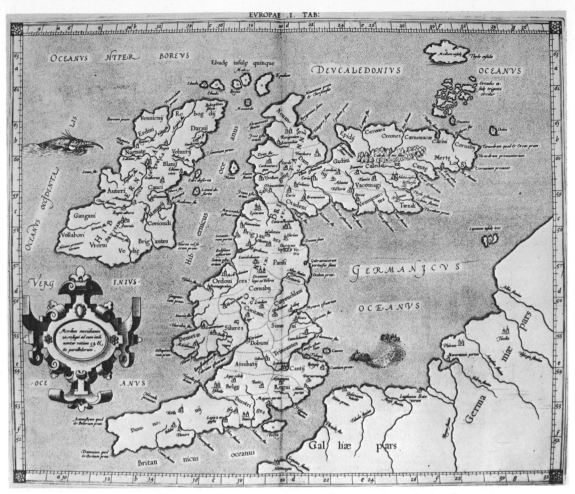

initials, *P* in Pretannic and *C* in *Cruithni*, is explained by the fact that at some point – one tentative date is 700 BC – one group of Celtic-speaking peoples, for whatever reason, came to substitute *C* for *P* at the beginning of words. Welsh and Breton are the survivors of the *P*-group and the Gaelic languages of the other. It is probable that in spite of this and other divergences, the two groups were still mutually intelligible at the period of the conquest of Britain, at which time, of course, the archipelago was predominantly Celtic in language and culture, as were Gaul and the Iberian peninsula. In Ireland it seems to be established that there are a number of homely words associated with fishing and husbandry which are excluded from learned usage and which are *P*- as distinct from *C*-words; this gives us the picturesque hypothesis of a dispossessed and oppressed *P*-group.

We now come to the period in which tribal conquest-migrations can be historically established. Most notable is that of the Belgae in

Ptolemy's map, in a 1618–19 edition, of Hibernia and Albion. This is, of course, a Latin translation of the second-century Greek original

the first century BC from north-eastern Gaul to south-east Britain and later to Ireland, to become, we believe, the *Fir Bolg* of the invasion traditions, but the practice continued down to the fifth century AD. Agricola considered the subjugation of Hibernia from Roman Britain, but thought better of it. Against this background the 'Book of the Invasions', *Lebor Gabála*, with its allied cycles of myth and hero- and king-tales, in spite of all its artless artfulness, begins to look a lot more plausible. In Ireland, by the time of Christian records, a linguistic and dynastic ascendancy had been established over the continuing conflict, but an innate sense of the fitness of things required that the new collectivity should also have its invasion/origin legend. So the name *Gwyddel* – Irish *Goídel*, modern English *Gael* – which was employed by literate Welsh-speaking missionaries to designate the population of the island as a whole, became the name of a fictitious eponymous ancestor and has been worn with pride by Irishmen of Gaelic allegiance ever since.

Our knowledge of the structure of the underlying units which went to make up this collectivity is surprisingly detailed, coherent and precise. The customary law of the Celtic peoples was highly developed and transmitted orally, apparently with extreme accuracy, from generation to generation by professional jurists. These were passionate casuists, conservatives and archaizers who, with the poets, historians and druids, as also smiths, artificers and musicians, formed part of the *aes dána*, the professional class. So tenacious was the system's hold on the Irish consciousness that it continued to function effectively – in theory sacrosanct, an immutable canon with which Christianity itself could not conflict, but no doubt in practice with many modifications and compromises – wherever the native power prevailed up to the time of the Tudor conquest. It is the 'Brehon Law' of Irish school history-books, a name derived from the Irish word *brithem*, 'judge', the title borne by its practitioners.

Under this law a man's identity was defined in terms of tribe and family; outside the tribe he had no legal personality. Only the men of art and learning passed freely between peoples. Land was the common property of the family and could not be alienated by an individual. Monarchy was elective within an extended family group. Wealth was reckoned in cattle. Slavery was practised. Honour – or 'face' – was assessable in concrete terms of livestock or chattels. Killing might be compounded by a blood-price. Custom and ostracism were the only express sanctions, but they were often reinforced predictably by *force majeure*. Cattle-raiding and warfare between kingdom and kingdom, with their shifting patterns of alliance, were an essential part of the political equilibrium, but it

must be remembered that in many cases the wars were highly formalized and may have involved no more loss of life than a faction fight at a fair in the eighteenth century or a riot at a football match today. To a great extent the unfree elements of the population, responsible for the servile work, and the commoners who tilled the soil did not take part.

We may judge from the descriptions in the literature that the homes of the Iron Age Irish were essentially similar to those of the early Christian period, of which many thousands of examples are known. Towns and villages did not become a part of the scene until after the Norse raids and settlements. The isolated rural homestead was the characteristic dwelling; it is still a feature of the Irish countryside. The enclosures, domestic or defensive, are the earthwalled raths and stone-built cahers and cashels, the ubiquitous 'fairy forts' of Irish landscape and folklore; the houses themselves would have been mainly of wood. The breathtaking drystone strongholds which dominate the cliffs of the western seaboard remind us that the geographical configuration of the country, making for cultural unity throughout the central plain, also provided refuges

The promontory fort of Dunbeg. Its drystone walls, perched 500 feet above the sea on the Dingle peninsula, were probably built in the early Christian period

19

The hill-fort of Ailech, Co. Donegal, is 17 feet high, $77\frac{1}{2}$ feet across. From the fifth to the twelfth century it was the seat of the northern branch of the Uí Néill dynasty

Iron Age (probably first century AD) snaffle-bit and decoration for horse-trappings. *Below:* bronze fibula, about third century BC. Both bit and fibula show traces of the red enamel that once filled in and emphasized their decoration

for dissidents along the rocky and mountainous coasts. The historical residences of the kings originated in this period and are almost invariably in close proximity to sanctuaries of the older ages. Almost certainly the worship of sacred stones persisted; they figure prominently in royal inauguration rites. Four of those known are enriched with the glorious floreate convolutions of La Tène carved ornament. St Patrick's great enemy was a divine personage called *Crom Cruach*, who was manifest in a standing stone addicted to human sacrifice.

Some authorities have contrasted the splendour of the epic descriptions with the relative simplicity of the way of life presupposed by the archaeological evidence. Many factors could be invoked to explain this discrepancy, most obviously the power of the creative imagination. Besides, in some cases, notably in those of the great circular erections associated with the traditional royal seats – which we know as 'hill-forts' although their purpose was as much ceremonial, we must believe, as warlike – the material remains are sufficiently impressive in themselves. We have also archaeological warrant from the Iron Age proper for much personal adornment, for the craft of enamelling, for the war-chariot and horse-trappings, for the sword and the trumpet – such swords and such trumpets as accompany in effigy the defeated Gauls of classical statuary. In later centuries, as the Empire recedes, a specifically Celtic art, reinvigorated and restored to dominance, emerges on the unconquered periphery of the British province. It flourishes in Ireland beyond the reach of the new Saxon invaders. The stage is now set for the coming of Christianity, and Ireland, which remained outside the Empire, comes to terms with Rome.

Decorated disk for the bell-end of a trumpet: probably first century AD

CHAPTER 2

Christianity to the coming of the Normans

One of St Patrick's seventh-century biographers, an Irish monk called Muirchú, writing in Latin, describes an encounter between Patrick and one Loegaire, *imperator barbarorum regnans in Temoria quae erat caput Scotorum . . . filius Neill, origo stirpis regiae huius pene insolae*, and this meeting has become a dramatic staple of the Patrick legend. It is not, however, an encounter that in any likelihood ever took place. St Patrick is, of course, a historical figure; he is indeed probably the least disputed historical figure we can produce for these islands after the withdrawal of Roman arms in the fifth century. His indomitable personality survives in records of his own composition. We have met the slave-owning, cattle-raiding Celtic chieftains in the last chapter and Patrick is a compelling witness that in his time their way of life continued unimpaired; he himself was captured as a boy in a raid on his native Britain and brought as a slave to Ireland. We know, in fact, a great deal about his personal life and the kind of world he lived in, but our only unchallenged date is 431. In that year Pope Celestine in Rome appointed a bishop named Palladius to the care of the Irish 'believing in Christ'. That Patrick's career belongs to approximately this period it is not reasonable to doubt, and it is customary to regard the recorded history of Ireland as beginning at this point.

We do not know the fate of Palladius's mission or how it dovetails with Patrick's, but of course the conversion of a people does not happen overnight and is not accomplished by one man. Two hundred years later there is still plenty of evidence of the tenacious fight put up by the old religion and also of missionary foundations other than Patrick's. It is noteworthy, however, that we have no records of martyrdom. As for the *imperator*, Loegaire, the 'High King' of later versions of the story, with his royal seat at Tara, we can only say that he represents the concept of the civil power that

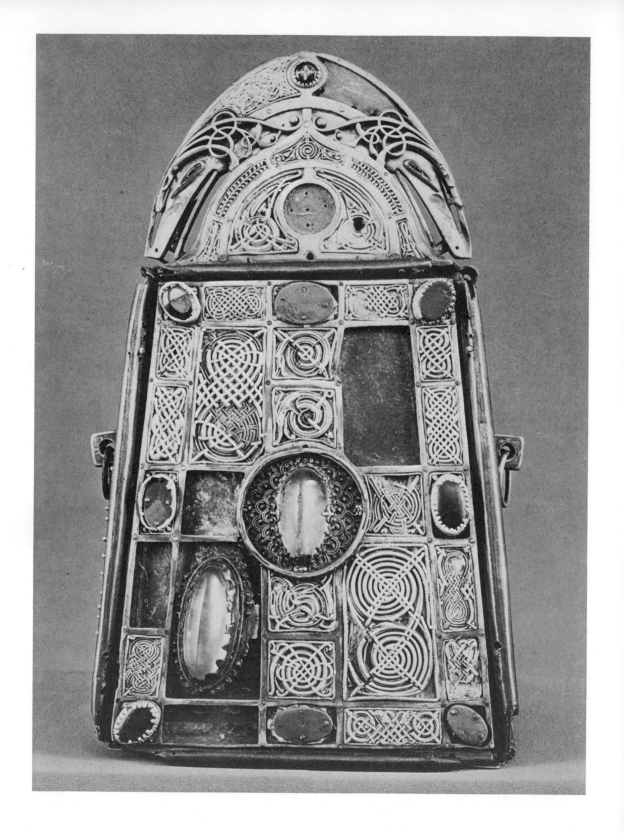

seemed fit and proper to a seventh-century monastic publicist writing two hundred years after the event. By the seventh century the idea of a single king claiming paramountcy over the entire island had come to seem a realizable ambition. In Patrick's time it does not appear to have been formulated even as an idea. The highest grade of king known to the laws is a *rí cóicid*, king of a 'Fifth' or province. Schematically there were five provinces of Ireland; politically the number varied. The most constant sub-division has been into the present four: Ulster, Munster, Leinster and Connaught. The claim to High Kingship, when it was made, was linked with the territorial possession of Tara. The principal claimants were the *Uí Néill*, the descendants of that Niall whom Muirchú names as the father of Loegaire and whose conquests won for him the surname 'of the Nine Hostages'. The Uí Néill had originally held the west and centre of Ireland to the south of Ulster, and it was not until the ninth century that one of their kings succeeded in taking the hostages both of the Leinstermen and of the ruling dynasty of Munster to become effectively king of the whole island. The ancient kingdom of Ulster, however, had fallen to them at an early date, and thereafter the fortunes of Armagh, St Patrick's ecclesiastical capital, are linked to those of Tara.

The great material change effected by Christianity was the introduction of the written word. The old insular Celtic culture had in fact been hostile to literacy, as being destructive of memory and concentration. A cumbrous system of writing did exist which could represent the letters of the Latin alphabet by what was basically a series of groups of short lines set at different angles on either side of a central spine. It was called *Ogham* and has survived mainly in tomb inscriptions on standing stones, but it could of its nature not have served as a vehicle for any sustained literary effort. The new learning was exclusively Latin, and traditional druidic or bardic schools existed side by side with monastic ones – initially almost certainly on terms of mutual abhorrence and distrust. Very early on, however, certain native professionals seem to have grasped the utility of the new technique. Characteristically, they made innovation the servant of conservatism, and the laws in their archaic incantatory form were committed to writing.

The Irish Christian schools were monastic, and so was the entire organization of the Irish Church. The Church Patrick brought to Ireland was organized on the Roman model with the control of administration in the hands of bishops. In Ireland, however, the Roman substructure of towns and cities was entirely lacking, and the model did not 'take'. The idea of the monastic 'family' on the other hand, which Christianity had also brought with it, was

Saint Patrick

Opposite: The Shrine of St Patrick's Bell: within this ten-inch-high, bejewelled and decorated casket, made *c.* 1091, is a plain iron handbell of the type in use in the earliest Irish Church, which may well indeed have belonged to St Patrick

This early Christian tombstone, from Aglish in Co. Kerry, is inscribed in the Ogham script, which represented the letters of the Latin alphabet by strokes or notches variously arranged on, and on either side of, a mid-line. At the head of the stone is the Celtic version of the Christian cross. Below that can be faintly seen two swastikas and a broad arrow; these are secondary. Around the edge, in the Ogham script, is the now almost indecipherable name of the dead man

readily assimilable. The monastery became the equivalent of the *tuath* or petty kingdom and functioned accordingly. The monastic grouping replaced the strictly territorial episcopal see. Bishops, as such, retained merely their sacramental functions. Nevertheless, the doctrinal purity which the Irish Church maintained in its considerable isolation is remarkable. Its main differences with metropolitan Rome were on this basic organizational level and liturgical. The Irish were extraordinarily and affectionately tenacious of old ways and, when the method of calculating Easter for use by the universal Church was changed in Rome, they found it very difficult to abandon the earlier method which they had received from so many revered teachers and founders. Records of the controversy remain, and it is impossible not to sympathize with the human dilemma of the 'Irish' party. It must, however, be made clear that there was also in Ireland at the time – the Roman Easter was accepted for these islands at the Synod of Whitby (664) – an innovating and reforming party at least equally typical of the forces within the Irish Church. For this civilization must not be thought of as mindlessly conservative. On the contrary, the ability to welcome what is new, to reconcile it with existing pieties and restate it in native terms is one of its most marked characteristics, and we can still call the seventh and eighth centuries, with wonder and delighted recognition, Ireland's 'Golden Age'.

The major reconciliation brought about by the genius of the period is that between the pagan and the Christian mind. Generations of Irishmen have known it personified in the much-loved figure of Colmcille, the 'Dove of the Church', St Columba. Like St Patrick, he is at the same time an authentic figure – his biographer Adamnán, writing at the end of the seventh century, is one of our rare trustworthy biographical sources – and a focus for a potent body of legend. He was born eligible for the Kingship of Tara; he became a mighty missionary abbot and established the Irish Church overseas in the Gaelic Kingdom of Dál Riada in Scotland from whence was initiated the evangelization of English Northumbria. His foundation of Iona rivalled the prestige of Armagh.

Tradition presents him as passionately devoted to learning and a master scribe – one of the most important functions of a monastery was, of course, the production of the manuscript books of the period – and the oldest surviving manuscript in western Europe is a psalter traditionally believed to be from his hand. Legend makes him a pugnacious as well as a gentle saint and it is perhaps not surprising that the little book should have been preserved by his tribe as a battle talisman, and come to be known as the *Cathach* or 'Fighting One'. It is a working psalter – very real and moving, very

The Dove of the Church

27

simple and very elegant. It dates from his time, is in the script of the
Irish schools, and may well be in fact his handiwork.

It was not only in the new learning that he was adept. He is said
to have been educated partly in a bardic school, and it is recorded
that poets were affectionately welcomed by him. This is the more
remarkable for the fact that the magical functions of the *fili* under
the pagan dispensation must still have been matters of living
memory. Colmcille becomes in Irish song and story the great advocate of the poets and of the native ways, their spokesman and defender. On his death the 'Chief-poet' of Ireland composed his
eulogy, the earliest piece of Irish verse whose authorship and dating
there is no reason to doubt. The alliance which has given us the
oldest surviving vernacular literature in western Europe had been
cemented.

For later Irish poets Colmcille stands also as the first and most
venerated representative of that extraordinary Irish manifestation,

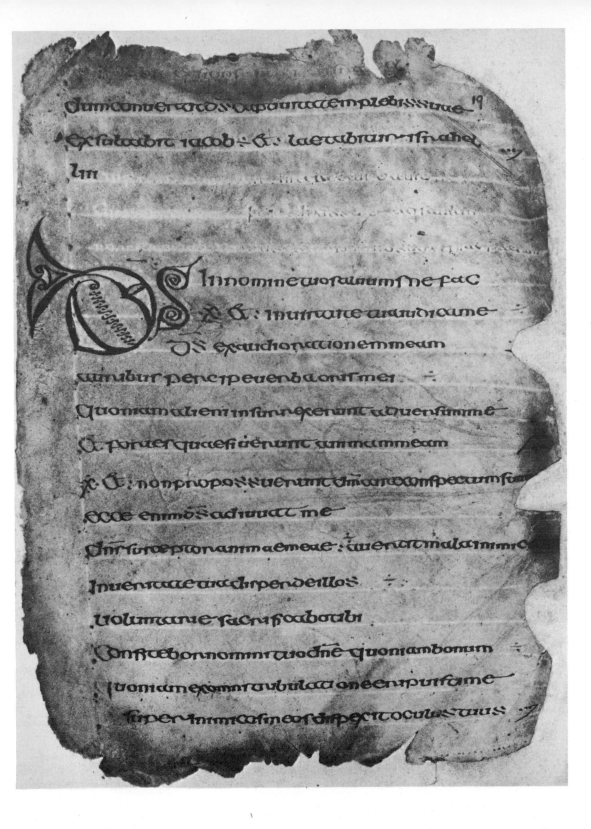

cum conuertit dns captiuitatem plebis suae

exsultabit iacob et laetabitur israhel

l111

In nomine tuo saluum me fac

et et in uirtute tua iudica me

ds exaudi orationem meam

auribus percipe uerba oris mei

quoniam alieni insurrexerunt aduersum me

et fortes quaesierunt animam meam

et et non proposuerunt dm ante conspectum suum

ecce enim ds adiuuat me

dns susceptor animae meae auertit mala inimicis

inuentate eorum disperde illos

uoluntarie sacrificabo tibi

confitebor nomini tuo dne quoniam bonum

quoniam ex omni tribulatione eripuisti me

super inimicos meos despexit oculus meus

the movement of the 'Exiles for Christ', and many set pieces on this theme are fathered on him. The essence of this exile was a bloodless or 'white' martyrdom, a kind of civil death. A man left his tribe, not only severing the links of natural affection, but abandoning everything that had constituted his secular identity, and sought some desert place where, living in austerity and prayer, he might be born again of Christ. The refinement of seeking not only physical isolation, but isolation *among strangers* rapidly followed. The impulse was initially not primarily a missionary one, but it came to play a significant part in the evangelization of the pagan peoples who had settled in western Europe in the centuries after the great breakthrough of the barbarians on the Rhine and the collapse of the Empire. The cells of these solitaries, and of the little communities of like-minded hermits that were a further development of their intent, are found in the most inaccessible and beautiful fastnesses of the Irish countryside and coastline. In Britain and on the Continent such men were torn between the claims of charity towards these foreign peoples and the contemplative life. Charity prevailed and schools and monasteries grew up about them, from Iona, Lindisfarne and Glastonbury in the west to St Gall, Bobbio and Vienna among and beyond the Alps.

The early monastery of Skellig Michael off the coast of Kerry: one of the 'communities of like-minded hermits' who sought out inaccessible fastnesses

Left: North door of the chancel, Iona Cathedral. This is part of a thirteenth-century Benedictine abbey founded on the site of St Columba's monastery

Below: The sixth-century monastic foundation of Devenish, on an island in Lough Erne. Round towers began to be built in the tenth century as belfries and refuges – the other remains are later

The Irish monks do not seem to have shared with many of the Fathers of the early Church the fear of 'the temptations of grammar and the lure of Apollo'. Their Latin was singularly classical for the period. Some of them may even have known Greek. The dominant figure is Columbanus, a younger contemporary of Colmcille's. He stands for everything that makes the Irish Church not only a proudly conscious participant in a common European heritage, but a self-confident contributor also. His indomitable courage took him right across Europe, and the number of foundations tracing their descent from the houses he established runs into hundreds. Like a prophet in the Old Testament he rebuked and chastened kings and he championed the Irish observance on the Easter question against that most formidable opponent, Pope Gregory the Great. Several of his magnificent, forthright letters are preserved and also some Latin verse, including a boat song for his companions bending to their oars against the Rhine.

His monastic rule strikes modern students as repellently severe. We have, however, striking testimony that it represented an escape from the tyranny of custom and magic into a world of sanity and rational order. Nature was no longer menacing, and the Irish monks looked on creation with the enchantment of children emerging from a dark room. The brilliant, spontaneous little lyrics we begin to find, scribbled in commonplace books or jotted down in the margins of more orthodox texts, are not the productions of cowed and dispirited men. Sometimes there is only, as it were, a note for a poem: 'Pleasant is the sun upon the margin of this book, because it flickers so'; sometimes there is a finished jewel of several verses. The language is Irish; the metres are distinctively Irish forms of the Latin hymn metres. There may be elements in them of the old pagan seasonal rites, but the intensely personal and individual approach is of the new dispensation.

By the ninth century, Irish learning had achieved considerable recognition. At the court of Charlemagne it furnished masters for the Palace schools. Many of its practitioners were by that time more eminent for scholarship than for sanctity. The towering figure of Scotus Eriugena seems to take his place among them only by the accident of birth, so much does he transcend ages and origins. In general these men were professionals, not selfless 'Exiles for Christ'. Indeed, they had now a sound practical reason for leaving Ireland and the maritime areas as a whole: the era of Viking expansion had begun.

The Vikings came from the Scandinavian North. They were pirates and traders. Their advanced techniques of shipbuilding placed the entire known world, as far east as Moscow and Constantinople, within their range. The Ireland of the 'Golden Age' had been free from invasion since prehistoric times and Christian for three hundred years. Its material culture was not only literate and prosperous, it was extraordinarily creative artistically. The monasteries were not only themselves the patrons of artists, they were also the depositories of the secular treasures of kings. The Vikings fell on these privileged and undefended sanctuaries, towns in all but name, fired them – they were built in large part of wood – and stripped them bare. One particular manifestation of the Irish genius they were not interested in – the great illuminated manuscripts; they could not read. Many of these naturally perished, but enough examples survive to document for us the canons of design that scribe and metal-worker, and perhaps also painter and carpenter, shared. The most famous of these is the 'Book of Kells'.

The Irish polity rallied after the initial shock. The character of the attacks also changed; settlement succeeded raid. The Irish kings

The Oseberg ship (restored). The Vikings' high standards of ship design and shipbuilding put the known world within their range

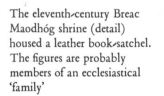

The eleventh-century Breac Maodhóg shrine (detail) housed a leather book-satchel. The figures are probably members of an ecclesiastical 'family'

The Ardagh Chalice, silver superbly decorated with gold filagree, coloured enamel and gilt bronze, dates from about AD 750. It is 7½ inches across at the rim

Opposite: Chi-Rho monogram (for Christus) from the Book of Kells. The intricate tracery of the decoration is typical of Ireland's finest illuminated manuscripts

built fleets against the invaders; the Norse built towns. Churches came to be built of stone and the lovely Irish belfry, the round tower, sprang up beside them to serve as a lookout point and place of refuge. Stone became the great medium of artistic expression. You cannot easily carry away a great stone monument like the Cross of the Scriptures at Clonmacnoise. The Norse towns and their hinter-lands – Dublin, and later, Limerick – achieved an uneasy status as client kingdoms after the Irish pattern. This was not without benefit to the country as a whole – Dublin minted the first coins in Ireland – but there is no Canute in Irish history. Indeed it is at this time, about 859, that an acknowledged effective High King emerges, in the person of Maelsechnaill, a prince of the Uí Néill. Irish king-ship, however, being not hereditary but elective, the paramountcy of the High King was strictly personal and had to be reasserted in arms by each new claimant, so that the long dynastic struggles were to continue as much a factor in the anarchy of the times as any Viking presence. The enigmatic Feidilimid, King-Bishop of Cashel, is said to have destroyed more churches than the foreigner.

The Uí Néill retained their pre-emption of the High Kingship for a relatively short time; the essentially disparate character of the power-structure militated against it. Their rise had created a vacuum in Munster and a hitherto obscure people, the *Dál gCais*, made themselves masters of the province. One of their princes was Brian *Bóroimhe* (Boru), and by 1002 he was undisputed High King of Ireland. His reign is unique not only because of his vertiginous rise to power but because of its extraordinary effectiveness. He saw him-

34

generatio

self as an Irish Charlemagne and thought in terms of institutions for the whole island. He confirmed Armagh in the ecclesiastical supremacy of the country, north and south. He restored communications and protected learning. The eleventh century was one of recovery and reform and the credit for their initiation is traditionally his. The final phase of the Viking wars may be taken as ending with his defeat of their forces at the Battle of Clontarf in 1014, where, at an advanced age, he met his death.

Significant is the fact that the Norse in this battle were the allies of the perennially rebellious Kingdom of Leinster, who alone among the Irish local sovereignties could claim they had resisted Brian's overlordship. Nearly one hundred and fifty years later we have the following entry in the great manuscript compendium now called the 'Book of Leinster': 'O King of Heaven, dreadful is the deed that has been perpetrated in Ireland today [the kalends of August], namely, Diarmait son of Donchad Mac Murchada, King of

Opposite: The Round Tower of Devenish. This closer view shows the height of the entry above ground-level – a usual feature of these places of refuge

37

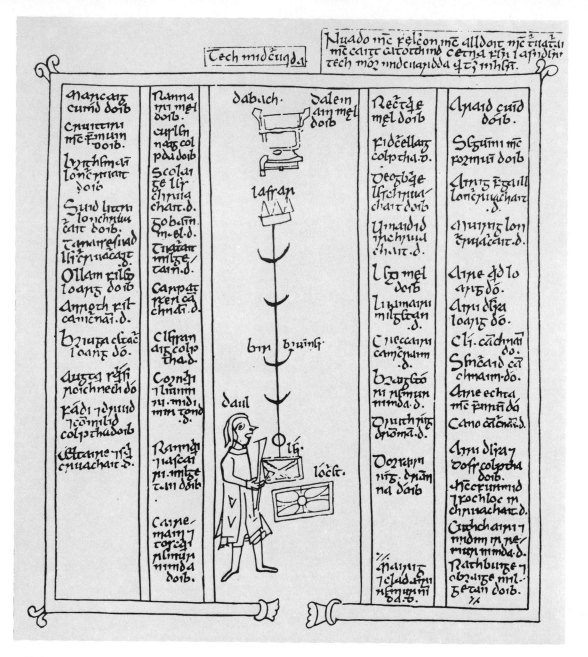

This imaginary ground-plan of the great banqueting hall of the legendary High Kings of Tara is found in the twelfth-century Book of Leinster

Leinster and the Foreigners [Dublin Danes], has been banished over sea by the men of Ireland. Alas, alas, O Lord, what shall I do?'

The King is Dermot Mac Murrough, the archetypal traitor of Irish popular historical convention, but the Leinster scribe clearly does not see him in this light; his consternation is occasioned by present loss rather than prophetic vision. The High King who banished Mac Murrough was Rory O Connor and the incident

38

Hiberno-Danish coin. Copied from a penny of Ethelred II (979–1016), it is one of the earliest coins to be struck in Ireland

must have seemed to contemporaries merely the latest development in the inveterate traditional struggle to impose the will of the High Kingship on Leinster. Dermot's feud with O Connor's neighbour, O Rourke of Breffney, whose wife he had abducted, had tipped the scale against him in the balance of alliances, but he was not the man to accept deposition or exile meekly. He looked for help to the Plantagenet Henry II, King of post-Norman-conquest England and Lord of the Angevin dominions in France. The politic Henry, intent on amassing kingdoms for his sons, had already given some thought to a possible conquest of Ireland and had taken the precaution of getting a bull of legitimation for this from the Pope, Adrian IV, the only Englishman in history to accede to the papacy. In return for Dermot's offer of fealty, Henry gave him licence to recruit among the land-hungry barons. It was a speculation in which he could not lose; at very worst it siphoned off turbulent vassals. By Irish usage, Dermot's oath would not be binding on his people beyond his own lifetime and he could in no circumstances alienate their lands. It was a situation which was often to be repeated and was to constitute fruitful grounds for reciprocal accusations of ill-faith between Gael and Englishman. Dermot found his allies conveniently near home among the marcher lords of the Welsh border; the forward edge of Norman dominion was about to be further extended.

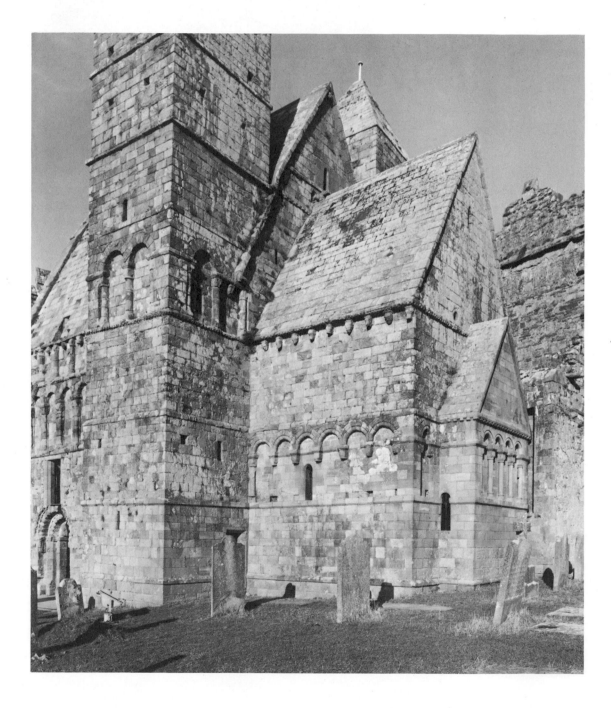

CHAPTER 3

A Conquest Absorbed

Pope Adrian's bull, *Laudabiliter*, authorized Henry II to undertake the conquest of Ireland with a view to remedying the deplorable condition of religion and morals. A generation or so earlier these papal strictures would have met with enthusiastic agreement from many Irishmen, notably the great reforming Primate of Armagh, Malachy. It was not only that the organizational peculiarities of the Irish Church or the permissiveness of the Brehon Law on the dis-solution of marriage appeared pernicious in the eyes of metropolitan Rome – the very real corruption and brutalization of the Norse wars took time to undo. By the middle of the twelfth century, however, reform was an accomplished fact and Ireland was in closer com-munion with Europe than she had been for centuries. The reunion is strikingly symbolized by the friendship between Malachy and St Bernard of Clairvaux, architect of the regeneration of European monasticism. Malachy died in the arms of Bernard and was buried wearing his habit. Bernard, when his time came, was buried in the archaic habit of the Irish saint.

The new order was accompanied not only by the importation of styles and ideas in many fields – among others architecture – but also by a sophisticated and conscious interest in the immemorial native culture. Saga and tradition had become not only the province of specialists but the recreation of scholarly amateurs. A letter to the scribe of the 'Book of Leinster' speaks eloquently for the gentle antiquarianism of the time:

Life and health from Finn, bishop [of Kildare] to Áed mac Crimthainn, lector of the high king of Leth Moga . . . and prime historian of Leinster in wisdom and know-ledge and book lore, and science and learning. And let the conclusion of this little tale be written for me accurately by thee, O acute Áed, O man of stately form. Whether I be a long or a short while away from thee my desire is that thou shouldst be with me. Let the poem-book of Mac Lonáin be brought me that we may discover the meaning of the poems that are in it. Et Vale in Christo.

Opposite: Cormac's Chapel at Cashel, Co. Tipperary, first of the Irish Romanesque churches, built 1127–34 by Cormac MacCarthy, King of Munster, who brought masons from the Continent for the work

We learn that Úa Crimthainn belonged to a monastic community of the old dispensation; Finn we know to have been a reforming bishop. Whatever lingering opposition this represented, it is clear that it did not prevent an affectionate literary collaboration.

'The Land of Ireland is sword-land,' wrote a sixteenth-century Irish court poet for a Norman patron in legitimation of the situation as it had by then evolved. The Hiberno-Norman lords, Butlers, Burkes, Fitzgeralds, nominally vassals of the English Crown, held by the sword the lands their fathers conquered, and ruled for all the world like those Irish princes whose power had weathered the invasion. The institutionalized spoils system at the base of Irish society powerfully influenced the course of events by making concerted resistance psychologically difficult and favouring individualistic aggression. Apart from this essential lack of concern for territories other than their own the Irish chiefs had other disadvantages in the struggle: their style of warfare had become archaic and formalized: they considered armour ungentlemanly and went into battle wearing only a linen shirt. Dermot's chief ally, the Earl of Pembroke, picturesquely surnamed 'Strongbow', was promised the King's daughter in marriage and the succession to the kingdom of Leinster, an arrangement which might well have founded a dynasty had Strongbow not died leaving no heir. His companions in arms went

Above: Irish foot-soldier of the time of Edward I. *Below:* The tomb of Strongbow, the Earl of Pembroke, in Christ Church Cathedral, Dublin

on to carve out 'kingdoms' of their own, and these initial successes were such that Henry II took fright and came himself to Ireland, accompanied by a considerable force, to forestall any secession. Reasoning from similar premises, many Irish chieftains and the Irish hierarchy did homage to Henry in return for his guarantee of their interests. None of the parties to these proceedings intended more than nominal adherence to them.

The Normans continued to thrust deep into the country, settling and fortifying, first with earthwork and palisade, later with stone-built castles. Henry concentrated on securing his share of the spoils and on retaining the loyalty of the towns. The Irish resistance remained ineffectual and within a hundred years of the first landing all seemed set for the permanent establishment of a prosperous English colony. It was at this point that the tide quite startlingly turned.

The defeats and retreats of the Irish lords had been less disruptive of their way of life than one might expect, affecting only the noble class with its retainers and men-at-arms and, most importantly,

The so-called 'King John's castle' at Carlingford, built by Hugh de Lacy in the twelfth century: a typical Norman fortress

English colonizers

43

Even in Elizabethan times, the Irish chief still lived a semi-nomadic, outdoor life

Monk writing, illustration from the manuscript of a thirteenth-century account of Ireland

its poets. The tillers of the soil, free or unfree, as a matter of course remained behind to work for their new masters. The Irish chief, even a great king in the heyday of his most settled power, was still a semi-nomadic person, who spent long stretches of his life in the open air, on progress or campaign, hunting or, in earlier times, quite simply on the move with his herdsmen as his cattle changed pasture. Habitually he dined out of doors after the fashion of the Fenian legends. He continued to do so into Elizabethan times to the great scandal of English observers who also found his diet, of under-cooked meat, raw salads, milk products and little or no bread, an abomination. If forced to 'take to the woods' his immediate material circumstances might change very little; his people bore the brunt of the reverse. It was a system that made for resilience.

One result of elective monarchy was that a generation or so in relative obscurity and a sweeping return to greatness were part of the norm for most chiefly families and it was the function of their poets to keep the prospects of recovery constantly present to their minds. Several major pitched battles ending in crushing Norman defeats mark the change and there is evidence that the Irish now thought in terms of a unified struggle. The crown of Ireland was offered in 1263 to Haakon IV of Norway, who died before he could accept, and later (1318) to Edward Bruce. Edward's advent forced the colony to realize its precarious tenure. A dissident Ireland presented a direct threat to the English Crown and a ready source of comfort to the King's foreign enemies. These considerations ensured a

44

Scenes from Richard II's campaigns in Ireland. Here his forces, cut off from their commissariat, are saved by the arrival of three ships with rations. Hungry soldiers wade into the sea

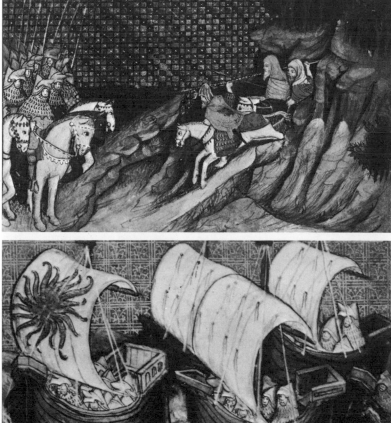

The Irish King of Leinster, Art MacMurrough Kavanagh, rides out from the woods for a parley with the Earl of Gloucester, Richard's envoy; note the Irish seat on a horse, without stirrups

The King sails for England at the end of his first expedition

steady flow of help, military and financial, to the infant parliament of the colony over the next hundred years, culminating in the two expeditions of Richard II, the second of which (1399) cost him his throne.

On the Irish side a counter to the Norman fighting machine had evolved. The north of Scotland and the Isles produced families of professional soldiery of Norse-Gaelic stock and these the Irish chiefs imported and settled on their lands. Highly specialized and heavily armed, they were known as 'galloglasses' (*gallóglaigh*, or 'foreign troops'). Another and even grimmer ally fought on the Irish side; in 1348–49 the Black Death struck Ireland and decimated the colony. By the early years of the fifteenth century the King's writ ran only in the walled towns and in the English 'Pale', a narrow strip about thirty miles long by twenty deep along the east coast, immediately surrounding Dublin.

The pressure of these events was heaviest on the townspeople and yeoman settlers. The Hiberno-Norman lords, by contrast, throve. The Irish resurgence had made them indispensable to the Crown and the creation of the three great earldoms, Desmond (Fitzgerald), Ormond (Butler), and Kildare (Fitzgerald), towards the middle of the century sealed the King's admission of this fact, but the forfeiture and outlawry only very shortly afterwards of the first Earl of Desmond demonstrates how dubious their surety could be. Indeed, the King's subjects in the colony complained only less of the exactions of the great earls than of the depredations of their Irish counterparts. They saw with horror their natural defenders, often the King's deputies, become daily more hibernicized, not only in language, dress and custom, but also in blood. From the very outset the Norman knights had intermarried with the Irish and were quick to grasp the political usefulness of a custom such as fosterage, under which the children of noble houses were brought up from infancy in other noble families with whom it was desirable to cement alliances. *Hibernicis ipsis hiberniores* ('more Irish than the Irish themselves') was no empty tag. The famous Statutes of Kilkenny proscribe in painstaking detail all manifestations of the Irish way of life by the King's English subjects, but they were a dead letter from the day they were drafted – in London! Perhaps they had a reassuring effect at home on the English backers of the colony. Almost two hundred years later, when Henry VIII was proclaimed King in the Irish parliament, the proclamation had to be read in the Irish language as, it was claimed, only the Earl of Ormond, the leader of the 'English' party, could understand it in the original.

The Hundred Years War and the Wars of the Roses in turn meant that no English king up to Henry VIII could give his indi-

Unified resistance

Opposite: On the charter roll of the city of Waterford is this portrait of the king who granted the charter, Edward III. In his reign, Ireland's population was decimated by the Black Death

47

vidual attention to Ireland, much less finance a reconquest. The Yorkist cause was indebted to the Desmonds, who in 1462 had routed the Lancastrian forces led by their rivals of Ormond. It was the zenith of the Desmond power, but six years later too close an association with the native Irish brought the Earl to the scaffold, and the King was forced to fall back on the other branch of the Fitzgerald family, that of Kildare. The Great Earl of Kildare became for over thirty years the uncrowned King of Ireland, in spite of a brief interlude at the Lancastrian restoration when Sir Edward Poynings (1495) effectively subordinated the business of the Irish parliament to the English Crown. The Great Earl was succeeded in his functions by his son Garrett Óg ('the younger') who in time came to fall foul of Henry VIII.

Peaceful development

History never consists entirely of alarums and excursions. Overall peaceful development in contemporary Ireland probably compared favourably with that in other countries. The dispersed nature of government ensured long spells of tranquillity even while isolated local magnates were engaged in feud or repression. The townsfolk of the colony were expressly permitted by law to deal with the 'mere' Irish, while the Irish lords built tower-houses on the Norman model and imported masons from the Continent. Their churches and cloisters west of the Shannon are gentler, more elegant than the grim Anglo-Norman Gothic of the east coast. On occasion they travelled abroad and wore English or European dress. Their libraries included texts in Latin and other languages as well as Irish.

The most striking achievement of their culture was undoubtedly its vernacular literature, which used for more than three hundred years a standard language of extraordinary economy and beauty. Irish poets seem to have retained to the very end their quasi-magical function; their praise was essential to legitimate rule and their satire was dreaded as a material threat. The Elizabethans, more perceptive than later critics, feared them as witches and hanged them as fomenters of treason. But it is clear that their official productions, in metres of remarkable and delicate complexity, recited to the accompaniment of the harp, were also the object of considerable aesthetic appreciation. We may deduce this from the excellent personal poetry by noble amateurs which survives. Probably the hibernicized Norman gentry began the practice – the Irish may have been restrained by remnants of superstitious awe. Such a literary convention indicates an absence of pressure which may also account for a certain aristocratic lack of ambition. We suspect that warfare was not too serious when we find the poet Earl of Desmond addressing a letter of apology in verse to his Irish friends for mounting an expedition against them, pleading in extenuation that if he failed to do so the

Opposite: A fourteenth-century carving of a noble-woman (perhaps the first Countess of Ormond) in St Mary's Church at Gowran, near Kilkenny

Athenry Castle, Co. Galway, built by the de Berminghams in the thirteenth century: a fine example of the tower-houses built by the Norman lords and soon copied by the Irish

King would hale him off to London and the Tower and so deprive him of the pleasure of their company. A Gaelic poet and scholar-king of Donegal, Mánus O'Domhnaill (1539), could think in terms of a Fitzgerald, that is to say Norman, kingship of Ireland. There was a power vacuum which Tudor monarchs were both too rapacious and too intelligent to ignore.

Edward IV had chastised Desmond; Henry VIII broke the great house of Kildare. The issue of Pope against King appears here as a rallying-cry for the first time in Irish politics. Church government, like the civil state, had been up to this time very much a matter of compromise and extemporization. The mendicant friars supplied in practice for many of the deficiencies of a disrupted or unassimilated organization, and the people as a whole could not be brought

The churches and priories west of the Shannon (*above*, Rosserk Abbey, Co. Mayo) were gentler, more elegant than the Anglo-Norman Gothic of the east (*below*, Fore Abbey, Westmeath)

to see the Church as oppressive. The Kildare heir, 'Silken' Thomas, now became understandably zealous for the papal over-lordship of Ireland. His rebellion was suppressed with hitherto unexampled ruthlessness, and advice was not lacking to extend this severity to the entire island. However, whether for lack of funds or from some real magnanimity, or deterred by the threat to place a Fitzgerald on the Irish throne, the King still sought to temper force with persuasion. His policy of 'surrender and regrant' induced the Irish lords to make over to him the title to their lands and receive it back at his hands on feudal terms. Several new earldoms were created. In Irish eyes their Earls had had no legitimate estate in what they 'surrendered'.

Nevertheless, the belief that the Irish might be won over persisted and the practice grew up of educating young men of noble birth at the English court. One of these was Hugh O Neill, subsequently Earl of Tyrone, the last great independent figure of the Gaelic order. His Renaissance single-mindedness and cunning in no way changed his basic acceptance of his Irish role as candidate for elective rule, a *rí-dhamhna* or 'material for a king'. A king in effect he became. Ulster, because of its topographical inaccessibility, had virtually escaped Norman dominance; the Earl dealt direct with Queen Elizabeth and ruled as his ancestors had done 'before the coming of Christ'.

The oldest surviving Irish harp, popularly known as 'Brian Boru's Harp'. Expert opinion dates it as not earlier than the fourteenth century

CHAPTER 4

Protestant Conquest

In the autumn of 1580 a Spanish and Italian force of some six hundred men, which had landed at Smerwick on the Dingle peninsula, the extreme south-west tip of Ireland, was besieged by an English force under the Lord Deputy, Grey of Wilton – Queen Elizabeth's representative in Ireland – who had with him his secretary, the poet Edmund Spenser. At a parley, a spokesman of the besieged 'avouched that they were all sent by the Pope for the defence of the Catholica Fide'. Lord Grey, as he reported to the Queen, 'marvelled' that such men 'should be carried into such unjust, wicked and desperate action by one that neither from God nor man could claim any princely power or empire, but indeed a desperate shaveling, the right Antichrist and general ambitious tyrant over all right principalities, and patron of the *diabolica fide*. . . .'

Edmund Spenser the poet, secretary to the Lord Deputy

The Pope's invaders, faced with the English artillery, laid down their arms. Then, Lord Grey's report goes on, 'I put in certain bands who straight fell to execution. There were six hundred slain. . . .' Lord Grey was already noted for his 'fervent zeal' for Reformation principles. He was, in fact, an early type of Puritan, and something of an extremist by the standards of Elizabeth's court. His action at Smerwick did not escape criticism. But Spenser warmly defended him, both for this action and for his general policy of ruthlessness against Irish rebels and their friends. Spenser urged a thorough reformation in Ireland, both religious and civil, and saw it as necessarily a reformation by the sword. He knew the human cost of such a war: the most vivid description of Munster after the crushing of the Desmond rebellion (1579–83) is from his pen: 'Out of every corner of the woods and glens they came creeping forth upon their hands, for their legs would not bear them; they looked like anatomies of death; they spoke like ghosts crying out of their graves; they did eat the dead carrions, happy where they could find them; yea and one another soon after, insomuch as the very carcasses they spared not to scrape out of their graves. . . .' For these horrors, however, the conquered, not the conquerors were responsible, Spenser thought: the Irish died 'of famine which they themselves had wrought'. After his own house at Kilcoleman had been burned by the Irish rebels, he considered, but reluctantly rejected, a final solution of the Irish question: 'How then? Should the Irish have been quite rooted out? That were too bloody a course: and yet their continual rebellious deeds deserve little better.'

Spenser had a personal interest in the matter; he was a settler. But he was also a humanist, on this precarious verge. Where Grey wanted to make Ireland safe for the Reformation, Spenser's kind of Reformation included the extirpation of popery, but in order to make way, not for some kind of rule of the saints, but for what he called 'sweetness' and 'civility': that is, for the values and order of the Renaissance. To what there was of sweetness and civility in the Gaelic world Spenser was almost deaf, since he did not know Irish. He had had Irish poetry translated for him, and granted it a savour of 'sweet wit and good invention', but his comments suggest that he believed it to be artless, as might be expected of a wild people, instead of being, as it then was, artful to excess. The wildness he saw, and feared: customs which had come down from the ancient

The Irish were constantly in revolt against English rule throughout Elizabeth's reign. Here Turlough O'Neill, leader of a revolt in Ulster, submits to Sir Henry Sidney. Behind him are his long-haired 'wild Irish' subjects

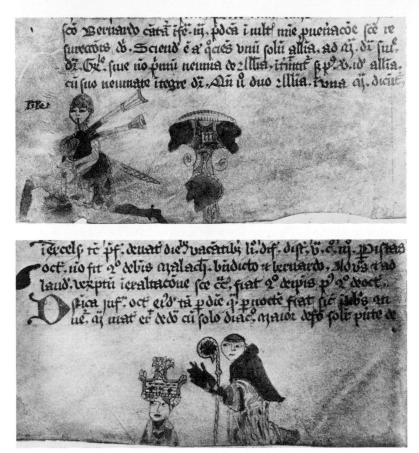

world mocked and menaced his hard-won civility. He witnessed
the execution of Murrough O'Brien at Limerick, and saw how 'an
old woman, which was his foster-mother, took up his head whilst
he was quartered, and sucked up all the blood running thereout,
saying that the earth was not worthy to drink it...'.

By Spenser's standards, to behead and quarter Murrough was not
barbarous, but to drink his blood *was* barbarous, and invited such
further beheadings and quarterings as might be necessary to put an
end to such practices and establish a civil Ireland, subdued and
largely settled from England. There can be no doubt that Spenser
and his friends genuinely conceived themselves to be engaged on a
mission of civilization, and they felt their own landed acquisitions
to be a legitimate reward for their part in this mission. The conquest
of Ireland provided the psychological basis, as well as a part of the
material basis and training, for the colonization of a great part of the
world. The young captain of 'certain bands' referred to by Lord
Grey at Smerwick was to be the great Walter Raleigh who planned
the first English Colonies in America.

The Gaelic order – together with such of the older English settlers as had accommodated themselves too well to that order – was now doomed, through the convergence on it of overwhelming forces. Renaissance ideas of order and civility, and zeal for the Reformed faith, were among these forces, but the most urgent drive came from another force, allied with those but distinct: the nationalism of a menaced England. Henry VIII had himself proclaimed King of Ireland in 1541, but did not securely establish English rule. The Protestant reforms carried out under Edward VI had not been enforced in Ireland, and under Mary – although a major 'plantation' or colonization took place in King's County and Queen's County (now Leix and Offaly) – England's control over Ireland further weakened. Thus on the accession of Elizabeth to an insecure and threatened throne, Ireland presented an opening to the enemies of the Queen of England, and of the Reformation. To pacify it was felt to be a necessity of national survival: and pacification required the destruction of the Gaelic order whose forms of liberty were, in English eyes, anarchy – Spenser complains of the freedom of Irish manners – and did in any case leave open doors to Spain.

Elizabeth herself had no enthusiasm for conquering Ireland – a costly and discouraging task – but her situation required this to be done. The Reformed faith had made hardly any progress among either the Irish or the older settlers – the 'Old English' as they were called. The devoted missionaries of the Counter-Reformation, on the other hand, found ready ears, and among their themes were the illegitimacy of Elizabeth and the duty of deposing her. It became necessary for Elizabeth's generals to fight four wars in Ireland: all of them involved a hope, and the last two the reality, of intervention by England's continental enemies.

The first rebellion was in Ulster, led by Shane O'Neill (1530–67), 'a great man, as savages go', according to G.R. Elton. It petered out on the death of Shane in 1567: the help sought from Rome and from France did not arrive. Rebellion then broke out in Munster, under James FitzMaurice FitzGerald, the 'arch traitor'; this was crushed in 1572, and FitzMaurice left for the Continent, where he is reported to have offered the crown of Ireland first to Henry III of France, and later to Don John of Austria. He was to return to Ireland with the Smerwick expedition, already referred to, and he met his death there, though not with the main body. This was in the course of the third rebellion (the second in Munster), that of the Earl of Desmond, which ended with the death of the Earl in 1583. Spenser's description, quoted above, is of the state of Munster at the end of this rebellion. Desmond's lands were confiscated and 'planted' by a syndicate of which Walter Raleigh was the head.

A proclamation (*opposite*), setting forth in summary form a number of laws 'to be duely kept and observed within this Realme of Irelande', reflects the fact that English law was widely flouted

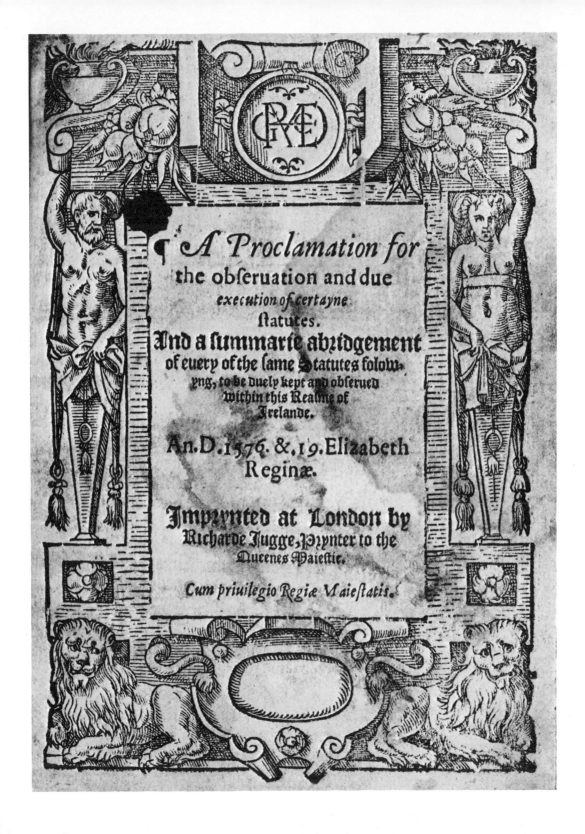

¶ A Proclamation for
the obseruation and due
execution of certayne
statutes.
And a summarie abridgement
of euery of the same Statutes folow-
yng, to be duely kept and obserued
within this Realme of
Irelande.

An.D.1576. &.19.Elizabeth
Reginæ.

Imprynted at London by
Richarde Jugge, Prynter to the
Queenes Maiestie.

Cum priuilegio Regiæ Maiestatis.

A noblewoman, a burgher's wife, and two 'wild Irishmen', from a contemporary Dutch description of the country

This Munster plantation was to be destroyed in the fourth, last and most serious of Elizabeth's Irish wars: that of Hugh O'Neill, Earl of Tyrone (1550–1616). Fighting began in Ulster, but after the Battle of the Yellow Ford in 1598 – the only major defeat for English arms in Ireland in this period – rebellion spread again; it was then that Spenser's house at Kilcoleman was burnt. The Earl of Essex, at the head of a large army, failed to cope with this dangerous situation and fell. It seemed at this point as if Ireland might be wrested from English control. Help arrived for the Irish from Spain; first money and ammunition, and for O'Neill 'a phoenix feather' (or peacock crown) from Pope Clement VIII; then in September 1601 a Spanish force of four thousand infantry under Don Juan de Aguila. But it was just a little too late. By this time Essex's successor, Charles Blount, Lord Mountjoy (1563–1606), had acted with great energy and largely redressed the situation. The

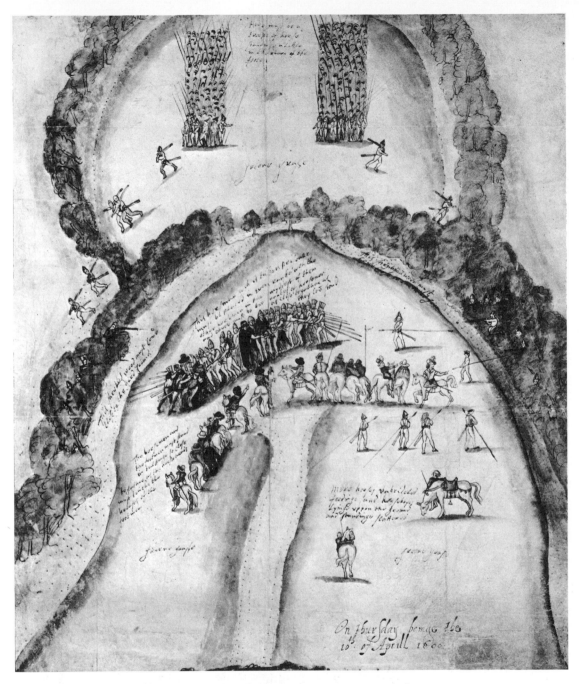

A setback for the Queen's forces: Thomas, Earl of Ormond, Lieutenant-General of her army in Ireland, is taken prisoner by the Irish forces under O'More

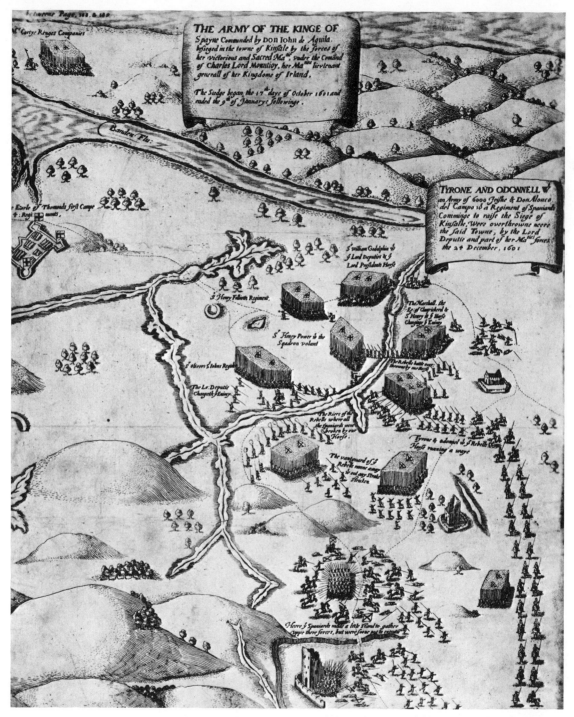

Help arrived for the Irish from Catholic Spain, including 4,000 infantry under Don Juan de Aguila. This force was besieged in Kinsale by Lord Mountjoy. The panorama above shows an attempt at relief by Tyrone and Red Hugh O'Donnell being put to flight (at lower right) on Christmas Eve, 1601

rebellion in Munster was over, but O'Neill and his young ally, Red Hugh O'Donnell, 'Chief of his name' (1571?–1602), made their way from Ulster to Kinsale, where they and the Spaniards were defeated by Mountjoy on Christmas Day 1601. O'Donnell fled to Spain, and met his death there, apparently by poisoning. Mountjoy invaded Ulster and destroyed the inauguration stone of the O'Neills at Tullaghoge. O'Neill submitted, and was pardoned by James, but lived in fear. On 14 September 1607 he and Tyrconnell, Red Hugh's brother and successor, Rory O'Donnell (1575–1608), sailed from Lough Swilly, never to return.

W.B. Yeats was to write of 'Four Bells – four deep, tragic notes in Irish history', each about the turn of a century. The first of these was 'the war that ended in the Flight of the Earls'. It is generally taken as signalling the death of the old Gaelic order, though in fact that order lingered on, rallying occasionally, for nearly a century more. But it had been very hard hit by Mountjoy, and it was never again to look as near ultimate success and secure survival as it had done immediately after O'Neill's victory at the Yellow Ford.

A pattern had now established itself that was to prove enduring: Catholic Ireland dominated by the superior force of Protestant England. Religion hardened, sharpened and preserved national animosities. Among the Irish a persecuted Church fanned the resentment of a conquered people: the English were heretics, their power was illegitimate, rebellion against them lawful, their enemies were the friends of Ireland and of the Faith. It was a vicious circle. English consciousness of these sentiments produced a feeling of insecurity in this quarter: the need for security produced strong measures, thus intensifying the Irish feelings at the root of the original feeling of insecurity, and creating the need for still further strong measures.

The Settlements

The best answer, from an English point of view, was to uproot the hostile native population, and replace them with loyal Protestants from England, Scotland and Wales: the method of 'settlements' recommended by Machiavelli in Chapter III of *The Prince*. Raleigh had tried and failed in Munster, Mary in the Midlands. The Flight of the Earls, however, cleared the way for a new plantation, this time in much more propitious conditions. The estates of the earls were declared forfeit to the Crown, and an effort was made, which was partially successful, to have a large territory – most of Ulster – settled from England and Scotland. If this policy had been consistently and generally applied, England could have solved its Irish problem. But in fact no policy was consistently applied over any long period; Ireland's affairs received only intermittent attention, perfunctory except in times of real danger.

Symbol of Protestant rule: design for a fort at London-derry

Archbishop Oliver Plunkett of Armagh. He died for his Catholic faith in 1681, after some years of religious tolerance

The conquest also created its own vested interests, not always coinciding with those of the dominant country. The 'undertakers' responsible for most of the Ulster plantation were supposed to have the natives completely removed from their lands; in practice they accepted Irish tenants, because it paid them better to do so. Ulster was to become, not a solidly Protestant province, but a province with two populations: Catholics and Protestants, mutually an-tagonistic, with religious animosity overlying the bitterness of a dis-pute over land. The Protestants of Ulster – and the much less numerous Protestants in the rest of Ireland – had, in a much more immediate and lively way, the same feelings of insecurity as English-men generally had about Ireland in critical moments, and they added their growing weight to the demand for strong measures.

Two Irelands, a Catholic one, still Gaelic-speaking, and a Pro-testant one, English-speaking and of mainly settler stock, were coming into being. Queen Elizabeth's foundation of Trinity Col-lege (1591), originally thought of as a bridgehead for the introduc-tion of 'civility' and Reformed faith into Ireland generally, became, by force of circumstances, the intellectual centre of a Protestant minority in Ireland: most of the Irish people were closed to it by the Counter-Reformation, as it was closed to them by the Reformation. In times when education was intimately associated with religion, a people that insisted on adhering to a religion opposed to that of their rulers was doomed to become an ignorant people, at least in terms of the learning prized by their rulers. Economically and socially, the conquest and its results depressed the condition of the native Irish: to all but a very few – those who made their way to the 'seminaries of treason' in Catholic Europe – the hope of a good or modern edu-cation was denied. This depressed condition increased, as it usually does, the contempt felt by the conqueror for the conquered, and the contempt in turn justified severity, which was felt to be brought on the conquered by their own inadequacies. 'These Irish', it was reported in 1613, 'are a scurvy nation, and are as scurvily used.'

The period from the end of the Elizabethan wars to 1641 was a period of relative quiet in Ireland, if we leave out of consideration the great plantations and the social disturbance they imply. Catho-lics during this period received a considerable measure of toleration. In principle the government of James I aimed at eradicating popery, but in practice the policy pursued was one of letting sleeping dogs lie. The Dublin government was instructed to 'forbear to make a curious and particular search for priests'. 'The Old English' – the Anglo-Irish gentry of the Pale – remained openly Catholic and were an important interest, even in Irish parliaments rigged to en-sure Protestant majorities.

In the next reign, during the vice-royalty (1632–40) of Thomas Wentworth, later Earl of Strafford, it was policy to play planters and papists off against one another, in order to achieve his purpose of turning Ireland into a secure basis of royal power and source of royal revenue. This looked promising, but ended in a double catastrophe. In Ireland these two factions briefly suspended the operation of their deep-seated hostility in order to make a tactical alliance against Strafford, supplying his English enemies with material for use in his attainder. In England, the suspicion that King Charles and Strafford intended to make monarchy absolute through the use of an army of Irish papists was among the most powerful factors working towards the discredit and ruin of the Royalist cause.

The relative religious tolerance which prevailed during this period was the result of state policy, not of any diminution in the mutual animosity of Catholic and Protestant. The plantations in themselves were enough to ensure a great intensification of these feelings; religion was now identified on one side with the desire to recover a territory and on the other with the desire to hold it. The

The ruins of Jigginstown House, Co. Kildare, built for Sir Thomas Wentworth, Charles I's deputy in Ireland

religions were different: the territory was the same. A good contemporary Catholic source describes the situation and state of mind
of the dispossessed:

They have no wealth but flocks and herds, they have no trade but agriculture or pasture, they are unlearned men, without human help or protection. Yet though unarmed
they are so active in mind and body, that it is dangerous to drive them from their an-
cestral seats, to forbid them fire and water: thus driving the desperate to revenge, and
even the moderate to think of taking arms. They have been deprived of weapons, but
are in a temper to fight with nails and heels, and to tear their oppressors with their
teeth. . . . Since they see themselves excluded from all hopes of restitution or compensation, and are so constituted that they would rather starve upon husks at home, than
fare sumptuously elsewhere, they will fight for their altars and hearths, and rather seek
a bloody death near the sepulchres of their fathers than be buried as exiles in unknown
earth.

These words of Bishop David Rothe were published in Cologne in
1617, long before the rise of Strafford. Their truth was to be proved

Scottish mercenaries in the service of Gustavus Adolphus of Sweden, 1631. The caption to this contemporary German broadsheet describes them as 'physically strong, enduring much: if bread be scarce, they eat roots'. The Irish 'galloglass' (see p. 47) came of the same stock

after Strafford's fall in 1641. In October of that year the Irish Catholics rose in arms; the main focus of the revolt was in Ulster – scene of the greatest plantations – but it was supported by the Irish generally. After some hesitation, the 'Old English' Catholic gentry joined it, so that the lines of a war of religion were set. Yet the war, which continued for more than a decade, was one of great political complexity. The different interests in Ireland – the native Catholic Irish, the 'Old English', the English Protestants, and the Ulster Scots – entered into shifting combinations among themselves, and with the contenders in the English Civil War. The leader of the 1641 Rising, Sir Phelim O'Neill (1604?–53), claimed to be acting under a commission from King Charles. The 'Old English' were generally Royalist. But the native Irish, though united to the 'Old English' by religion, felt no loyalty to an English Protestant king. They looked abroad for help in the usual quarters: Spain, the Pope.

Shortage of coin in Ireland in the 1640s led to the minting of so-called 'necessity money', crude lumps of silver stamped with their weight in penny-weights and grains

Little help came: some money, and much advice, of which the principal bearer was the Nuncio, Giovanni Battista Rinuccini (1592–1653), who arrived near the end of 1645. Charles's Lord-Lieutenant, James Butler, Earl of Ormond (1610–88), sought to enlist the Irish rebels in a common front against the Parliament, or at least to secure a truce with them. The Irish and 'Old English' were divided on this issue. Rinuccini threw his full weight against any truce with the heretic envoy of a heretic prince, and he was supported in this by the successful and popular Owen Roe O'Neill (1590–1649), nephew of the great Hugh and himself winner of the greatest Irish victory of this period, at Benburb in 1646, over Monro's Scottish Army. The quarrel between Royalists and Irish had not yet been fully resolved when both sides were crushed by Cromwell's Ironsides in 1649–52.

In retrospect, Ormond's policy seems sound, Rinuccini's perverse. The mild rule of an Ormond – especially an Ormond indebted to the Irish – should be greatly preferable, one might think, to the militant Protestant rule which a Puritan victory would certainly bring. The interest of the Irish Catholics may well seem to us now to have lain in the alliance with the Royalists against a common and deadly enemy. Yet there can be no doubt that the Irish generally did not see the matter in this light. They did not trust the Royalists, and with good reason: Ireland, King Charles had written to his wife in 1645, 'must at all times be sacrificed to serve the crown of England'. The Irish, of course, did not know that he had actually stated this principle, but they suspected his intentions. The Irish Catholics were also little disposed to make distinctions between Protestants: Charles, Ormond and Cromwell were all Protestants and there was felt, therefore, to be little to choose between them. The dispossessed Irish must also have known that a victorious king would be no more inclined to give back their lands than the Parliament would be: it was, after all, a king who had taken the lands away.

Finally, the Irish Catholics were not satisfied with the idea of being merely tolerated, which is all that Ormond could safely or plausibly promise. They wanted the Catholic faith established 'in its splendour', and heresy extirpated. This was Rinuccini's object, and Rinuccini, though detested by some of the lords, lawyers and gentry of the Confederation of Kilkenny – the Catholic Assembly – was venerated by the people. When he left Ireland in February 1649 – the leaders of the Confederation having repudiated him and his policy – he was accompanied to the ship *San Pietro* by a crowd of weeping people. He was impressed, and thought that the corrupted nations nearer Rome should 'journey to a distant clime where

Opposite: Parliament's forces, too, were short of money, and badly mismanaged, as this broadsheet shows, in a heart-rending catalogue of disaster and distress

66

The humble Petition of us the Parliaments poore Souldiers in the
Army of Ireland, whereof many are starved already, and many dead for want of Chirurgions,

Sheweth,

THat we the poor distressed Souldiery under the Parliaments Service in Ireland, having heretofore served the Parliament under the Lord Generall Essex, valiant Massey, and noble Sir William Waller, and the rest, &c. did in all faithfulnesse, hardship and desperate service as ever any, hazzard our lives and fortunes, and did according to order obey and disband then not so much as doubting of all our Arreares, and now have almost served you two years in all integrity and faithfulnesse both Winter and Summer, wet and dry, frost and snow, having no other bedding then the bare ground for our beds, and the skies for our covering, and when dry in the day and night, no other signe to drink at but the Sun and Moone, and nothing but water, having no plenty, but cold backs, hungry bellies, and puddle water, and when sore wounded, not a Surgeon to dresse us, or if a Surgeon, no chest, nor salve, nor oyntments; and for bread many times not a loafe of two pence under six pence, and rotten cheese sent not fit for a dog, and for butter it went from London to Dover, and mistook Dublin and went to Dunkirk, and for our new cloathes all made of the French fashion, and being too little for any of us, were carried for France to cloath them, hardly hats to our heads but what our haire growes through, and neither hose or shooes, doublet or breeches, tearing our Snapsacks to patch a hole to hide our naked and starved flesh, and our swords naked for want of scabberds : Thus with our backs without cloaths, and our bellies without food, and not a penny to buy any thing, and the Kernes having burnt the corne and destroyed all fit for succour, we forced to march bare legged and bare footed, having neither fire nor food, we perish in misery, and our Commanders being in a manner in the same case, having nothing but good words to pay us with, shewing us often your Orders upon Orders for our pay, plentifully promising but not performing; and thus wee dropping downe dead daily in our marching, and so feeble and so weak, being not able to fight or do any more service without some supply, but all like to starve and die in misery, when all meanes is anticipated, and the Tax of 60000.l. wholly ingrossed by your Army from us, and your Souldiery quartered in Kings. houses, and clad Gentile like, and fed in Free-quarter to the full, and lie in good beds, and take their pleasure and ease in rest and peace.

We humbly desire our hungry bellies may once be filled, and our naked backs be cloathed, and our legs and feet be hosed and shooed, and our Surgeons once more fitted, and all recruited with food to supply us once more, that we may go out again to finish that worke we have begun, and not to lie like Drones to eat up others meat, and we do not doubt, but with Gods blessing, to give you a happy account of the Conquest of the whole Land, and shall ever pray for a happy Parliament.

Feb: 18.   DUBLIN: Printed by *W. B.* 1648. 1647.

the sun is never seen, that they may fully comprehend the due sub-
jection of the faithfull to their head'.

In the conditions of the mid seventeenth century – granted the
relative strength of England and Ireland, and the unwillingness of
continental powers to intervene – to expect to secure an Ireland with
Catholicism 'in its splendour' was to expect a miracle. To expect a
miracle was, however, not extraordinary in the seventeenth century:
the clergy, the ordinary people, and such leaders as Owen Roe do
seem to have expected that God would grant his faithful achievements which to rational calculation would appear impossible.

Cromwell For the Irish, 1649 was the fatal year, not because of the execution
of Charles, but because of the death of Owen Roe, the departure of
Rinuccini, and the arrival of Cromwell in Ireland.

Cromwell, like most other Englishmen and all Puritans, had
been deeply shocked by what he had heard of atrocities against Protestants in the Rebellion of 1641. The actual facts about these atrocities are thus summarized by a fair-minded historian, Richard
Bagwell: 'Several thousand Protestants were massacred, not confined to any province or county, but occurr[ing] in almost every
part of the island...the retaliation was very savage, innocent persons often suffering with the guilty...great atrocities were committed on both sides.' In England, naturally enough, the anti-
Protestant atrocities had been widely publicized, with unrestrained
exaggeration, while nothing was remembered of the retaliation.
Cromwell and his comrades therefore felt fully justified in treating
the Irish rebels with the greatest ruthlessness, and such ruthlessness
could also meet a political need: to clear out the rebels and put
English ex-soldiers in their stead would serve the double purpose of
settling Ireland, and of removing a potential source of turbulence
from England.

From a military point of view, the ferocity of Cromwell and his
successors in Ireland, Ireton and Ludlow, was not extraordinary
by seventeenth-century standards. The action of Cromwell's which
lingers in the folk memory – the sack of Drogheda – was hardly more
ferocious or macabre than that of Cashel by Murrough O'Brien,
Earl of Inchiquin, in 1646. One may suspect that the real shock
administered by Cromwell came not so much from his cruelty as
from his efficiency, and above all from the determined and systematic character of his anti-Catholicism. To the Governor of New
Ross, who sought assurances for liberty of conscience, Cromwell
replied: 'I meddle not with any man's conscience, but if by liberty
of conscience you mean a liberty to exercise the mass, I judge it best
to use plain dealing, and to let you know, where the Parliament
of England have power, that will not be allowed of.'

By 1653 the Cromwellian forces had subjugated all of Ireland. Their leaders aimed at a lasting solution for the question, and had clear views how such a solution might be obtained. One of their most successful commanders, Michael Jones (d. 1649), had laid down that 'no lasting peace could be made but by removing all heads of septs and priests and men of knowledge in arms, or otherwise in repute, out of this land...'. In John Milton's opinion, the Irish were 'indocile and averse from all civility and amendment'. It was accordingly resolved to clear all the Irish owners out of all the good land in Ireland. To simplify a very complex settlement, those who could show that they had not been rebels might receive compensation out of rebel lands expropriated in the poor and rocky country beyond the Shannon; rebels lost their land outright, and in Ireland east of the Shannon their land went to Protestant settlers. Among the victors, at least one commentator questioned the wisdom and humanity of this general settlement. Vincent Gookin, a member of an Irish constituency in Cromwell's parliament, referred to 'the impossibility of this transplanting'. 'Can it be imagined', he asked, 'that the whole nation will drive like geeses at the wagging of a hat upon a stick?' 'It was their being cruel that makes us hate them so much!' he wrote. 'To punish them do not run into their sin, lest God punish thee.'

Portrait of an Irish chieftain, believed to be Sir Neill O'Neill (1658–90). The model may, however, be a contemporary actor, John Lacy. Compare the middle picture on p. 45

The transplantation was not in fact as thorough as seems to have been intended. The main reason was that the native Irish continued to be needed east of the Shannon as a labour force. Many thousands crossed the Shannon, and many tenants followed their landlords, but great numbers remained on their old land under new landlords. The most important effect of the transplantation was not a movement of population, but a great change in the ownership of land, and in the distribution of political power. What had been established over most of the island was in fact a landed ruling class, mainly of English and Scottish origin, professing some form of Protestantism and dominating a native Roman Catholic and still Gaelic-speaking peasantry. This was the Protestant Ascendancy, which lasted, in its essentials, into the last quarter of the nineteenth century. In eastern Ulster, however, Protestant ascendancy rested on the more secure base of a Protestant (settler) peasantry.

The Ascendancy

The Restoration made no substantial change in the Cromwellian settlement of Ireland. Charles II's parliaments restored some hundreds of persons to their old estates, and confirmed the new owners in the possession of the remainder. It has been estimated that Catholics held three-fifths of the land in Ireland in 1641; by 1665, on the completion of the Restoration settlement, they held one-fifth, mostly in Connaught. They benefited little from the improvement

Among the decrees issuing from the restoration of Charles II was this one, beautifully engrossed and elaborately decorated, for the 'better regulating of the art and mistery of coopering in our citty of Dublin'. It is now in the Guinness Museum

in the economy – the expansion of the export trade in beef, butter, hides, tallow and grain – which took place in this period. Six-sevenths of the population, according to Sir William Petty's calculation, continued to live at subsistence level growing their own food – mainly, by now, the potato – and weaving their own cloth. The native inhabitants were crushed, but not altogether quiescent. The 'tories' – outlaws drawn from the ranks of the dispossessed – threatened the new rulers and owners throughout much of the country. But in the more settled parts, the Ascendancy showed confidence in the future. Dublin began its great expansion, and Ormond, returning as Lord-Lieutenant, began to plan it on the stately lines of a Baroque city.

The accession of James II, an avowed Roman Catholic, inevitably raised the hopes of the dispossessed and alarmed the Ascendancy. These feelings were greatly intensified when a Catholic, Richard Talbot, Earl of Tyrconnell (1630–91), took office as Lord-Lieutenant in 1687. Tyrconnell raised a large and almost entirely Catholic army, part of which was called over to England by James.

The simultaneous arrival of armed Irish papists and of Protestant refugees from Ireland was among the most important factors in turning James's English subjects actively against him.

On 12 March 1689, James arrived in Ireland from France, where he had fled after the 'Glorious Revolution' of 1688 in England. His forces under Tyrconnell held all of Ireland with the exception of Enniskillen and Derry (Londonderry). James had with him diplomatic and military advisers from France: French troops were to follow. Internally, in Ireland, the situation was more clear-cut than it had been in the 1640s: it was a fairly straightforward struggle between Catholic natives and Protestant settlers: the Catholics relied on a Catholic king for the overthrow of the Protestant settlement of the 1650s. In Dublin, a Catholic parliament passed an Act confiscating the property of almost all the Protestants in the kingdom. The old distinction between those Catholics (mostly of 'Old English' stock) who were loyal to a Protestant king and those Catholics (mostly native Irish) who rejected such loyalty was rendered irrelevant by the new fact of a Catholic king assailed by heretics. Nor was there any nuncio, this time, to trouble counsels.

James, Earl of Ormond, raised to the dukedom on the Restoration, and appointed Lord-Lieutenant. He presided over the great expansion of Dublin, when the city gained stately buildings such as the Royal Hospital, Kilmainham (*below*)

This internal simplification had been effected by an external complication: the Pope was not, this time, on the Catholic side as far as the civil war in James's dominions was concerned. The quarrel between the Holy See and the French monarchy, over the question of the liberties of the Gallican Church, rendered impossible any Vatican support for Louis's protégé, James. In Ireland, the contending parties felt themselves to be fighting 'for' and 'against' the Pope, but the Pope was not in reality where he was expected to be. The fact remains an embarrassment to those on both sides who cherish simple historical pieties. In our time, the Parliament of Northern Ireland, which venerates the memory of the victory of Protestant William over Papist James, once acquired and displayed a portrait of their deliverer. The portrait was hurriedly withdrawn when one of the figures shown as hailing – and perhaps even blessing – the Protestant hero was identified as Pope Alexander VIII.

Louis, at war with the Emperor and the Dutch as well as with England, could spare little for war in Ireland. The Irish troops were numerous, and French bservers thought them promising raw

'James II appointed the Earl of Tyrconnell, a Catholic, as Lord Lieutenant — the "new deputy" mocked in the Protestant song *Lilliburlero*.

material, but they and their officers were mostly untrained and badly armed. Louis's War Minister, Louvois, foresaw the outcome, putting no confidence in miracles: 'Whatever good intentions', he wrote, 'the Irish may have for the preservation of their country and their religion, if they fight with three-foot sticks, against the troops of the Prince of Orange which will have swords and muskets, they will soon be killed or forced to fly.'

Derry was relieved by an English fleet on 28 July 1689, after a siege of fifteen weeks. Shortly afterwards Marshal Schomberg established a bridgehead for William of Orange in eastern Ulster, at Carrickfergus. There, William himself landed on 14 June 1690. On 1 July he defeated James's forces at the Boyne. James left Ireland a few days later for France, never to return to any of his kingdoms. He had conducted the struggle in a half-hearted manner; he must have known that the support he had won in Ireland, and the measures necessary to hold that support, were of a nature to damn his cause irrevocably in England – since his only loyal Irish subjects were England's irreconcilable enemies.

Richard Talbot, Earl of Tyrconnell

A Protestant playing card shows Tyrconnell "arming ye Papists". "Undaunted Londonderry", besieged by King James's forces, but relieved by King William, inspired further Protestant songs'.

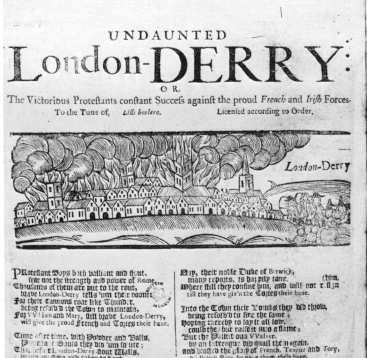

In June 1690, William of Orange landed in Ireland, and Catholic James's cause was lost. Defeated at the Battle of the Boyne (*above*), James took flight from Waterford (*below*) for France, where he died in exile, last of the Stuart Kings. Catholic resistance continued for a short time, but ended at last with the bombardment and surrender of Limerick (*right*)

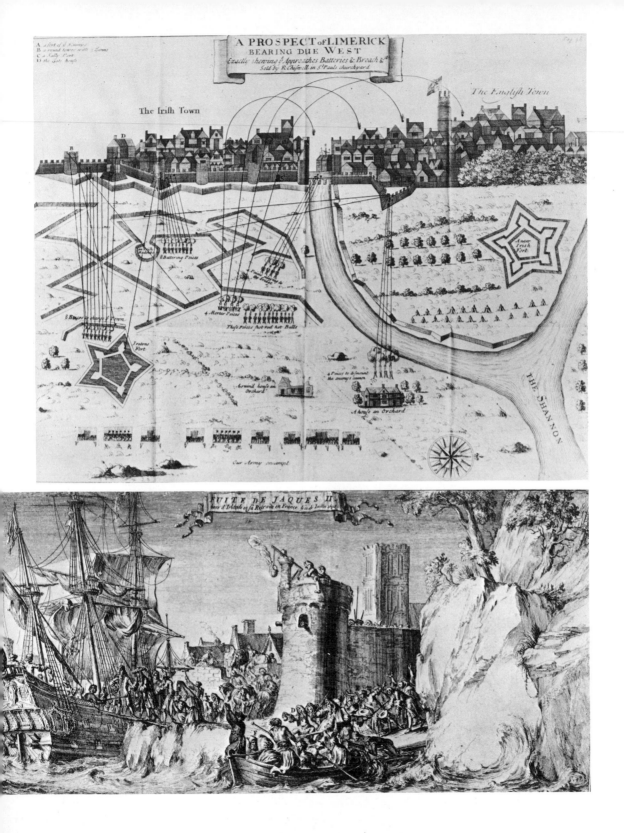

The Irish, with some French support, continued the struggle, in the midlands and in the west, for more than a year. Patrick Sarsfield (d. 1693) distinguished himself as a cavalry leader during this period, and remains one of the best loved of Irish heroes. Sarsfield surrendered the Irish stronghold, Limerick, on 3 October 1691, on terms (see p. 77). He and more than ten thousand Irish troops sailed for the Continent – the most famous flight of the 'Wild Geese', the Irish émigrés who made up an important part of several of the continental armies of the seventeenth and eighteenth centuries.

The Battle of the Boyne was the second of Yeats's 'Four Bells'. The Protestant conquest was now complete. The Catholic population was both crushed and hated by its masters, with what was felt to be a righteous hatred, which it fully but now silently reciprocated. 'Hatred answering hatred,' Lady Gregory was to write long afterwards, 'death answering to death through the generations like clerks at the mass.'

The tragedy could not have been averted, or even notably softened, by the wisdom or humanity of any ruler. The people of Ireland had been caught and crushed in the play of international and ideological forces: the English Reformation and its insecurity; the Counter-Reformation and its quasi-millennial hopes; the ambitions and fears of dynasties; the quickening consciousness of nationalism English and Irish, and economic interests and hopes both underlying and developed by this interplay of forces. English and Irish, pressed into closer contact by these forces, discovered how diversely history had formed them. Each side reacted to this discovery with that ethnocentric reflex of shock, disgust and anger, which is among the strongest and most terrible forces in human history. The weaker party was doomed to be oppressed, and the weaker party was the native population of the smaller and more remote island.

'Many (of them) are not equal to one (of us)': a medal struck to commemorate the Protestant victory

CHAPTER 5

Protestant Conquest Undermined

The terms on which the Jacobites surrendered Limerick stipulated a wide measure of toleration for Catholics in Ireland: Roman Catholics were to enjoy such rights of worship 'as are consistent with the laws of Ireland, or as they did enjoy in the reign of King Charles II'. William wished to honour this agreement, but the Irish parliament, representative of the Protestant interest so recently menaced, was bent on treating the papists as a conquered but still dangerous people, which should be deprived of the protection of the law. On this point, at this time, Irish Protestant opinion was supported by English Protestant opinion. William gave way. There began in his reign, and continued under Anne and the first two Georges, a series of anti-Catholic statutes: the Penal Laws.

Under these laws, Irish Catholics could not sit in parliament, or vote in parliamentary elections; they were excluded from the bar, the bench, the university, the navy, and all public bodies; they were forbidden to possess arms, or a horse worth more than five pounds. No Catholic could keep a school, or send his children to be educated abroad. The ownership of land was the subject of a whole complex branch of the penal code, as a result of which almost all the remaining land still owned by Catholics passed into Protestant hands. Division was fostered in Irish families by laws conferring extraordinary privileges on any member of such a family who became a Protestant – for example, the eldest son, by becoming a Protestant, could deprive his Catholic father of the management and disposal of his property. Catholic bishops and other higher ecclesiastics were banished from the country, and were liable to be hanged, drawn and quartered if they returned. A certain number of registered priests was tolerated, and unregistered priests were liable to the same penalties as bishops.

'Penal cross', dated 1712 – crudely carved memorial of a pilgrimage, an object of popular devotion at a time when such things were officially disapproved

77

Edmund Burke: detail from
his statue in front of Trinity
College, Dublin

The penal laws

According to Edmund Burke, the penal code was 'a machine of as wise and elaborate contrivance for the impoverishment and degradation of the people, and the debasement in them of human nature itself, as ever proceeded from the perverted ingenuity of man'. Burke, however, might be regarded as a prejudiced witness; his mother was a Catholic, and it is likely that his father, an attorney, had become a Protestant to escape the operation of the laws in question. It is possible to view the code more indulgently. Thus the eminent Victorian writer on the period, J. A. Froude, says that the laws affecting the Catholic clergy were 'justified by provocations with which no people in the world but the English would have dealt so forebearingly'.

The penal code was in fact a necessary consequence of the form which the conquest had taken. The native Irish were not to be altogether exterminated, for their labour was needed. At the same time, the vital interests of the settlers required that the natives should be allowed neither to repossess their lands, nor to put themselves in a position – through education, political activity, arms or alliance – where they might effectively threaten the land settlement. In England, as long as Catholicism was still felt as a real menace, Protestant opinion, and parliament, supported the settlers in this matter.

The code had, of course, an offensive as well as defensive significance: it extended the conquest, as well as preserving it. 'The penal code as it was actually carried out', wrote the liberal Anglo-Irish historian W. E. H. Lecky, 'was inspired much less by fanaticism than by rapacity, and was directed less against the Catholic religion than against the property and industry of its professors.' What the code did was to perfect and maintain a system of caste domination, with the superior and subordinate castes marked off by religious profession, and with different systems of law applicable to them. In a country in which three-quarters of the inhabitants belonged to a conquered population, it is hard to see how the conquest could have been maintained without some such system.

There are some resemblances between the penal code and the system loosely called *apartheid*, through which a conquering minority codifies its rule over a conquered majority in South Africa. There were, however, important differences. Religion is a much less stable and effective badge of caste than colour is. It was easy, materially speaking, for a Catholic to 'pass' if he wished to do so. The Protestant population became diluted by the addition of people who did not really share the feelings and tradition of the conquerors. Intermarriage had become common, and never altogether ceased, despite severe penalties at the height of the penal period. The most vociferous Protestant might well have Catholic cousins, and be less fierce

78

George Berkeley, Church of Ireland Bishop of Cloyne, with his family and friends. For all that he was a member of the ruling class and the established religion, he spoke and wrote vehemently against the wretched condition of the Catholic peasantry

in practice than in theory. The very fact that the criterion was one of religious profession – and therefore of voluntary application – made it impossible for the ruling caste to attain that implacable rigidity, due to a certainty of natural superiority, which is the heritage of the born racist. Racist doctrines – including the doctrine of the natural inferiority of 'the Celt' – did not become influential in Europe until a much later period: they may have been in part a substitute for a religious fanaticism which had become obsolete. Had the chronology of conquest been different, a penal code based not on religion, but on a theory of preserving the purity of the 'AngloSaxon race' from 'Celtic' contagion, might perhaps have produced a more enduring conquest. As it was, the application of the penal code was capricious: sometimes ferocious, often mean, but often halfhearted. With the spread of Enlightenment principles, and the growing incredibility of a Jacobite threat, the whole system became increasingly distasteful to educated Protestants, who often helped Catholics to evade the operation of the laws. The moral position of the mass of Catholics, refusing the material benefits open to them if they conformed, impressed some Protestants: Froude refers to 'the steady courage and unremitting zeal' with which the Catholics maintained and multiplied the numbers of their priests, despite the penal laws.

Despite the imperfections in the operation of the penal code, the consequences of total defeat weighed on the Catholic population

Jonathan Swift: 'all government without the consent of
the governed is the very
essence of slavery'

*Division among the
conquerors*

throughout the first half of the eighteenth century, and less heavily
for long thereafter. Gaelic poets expressed, in the form of the *Aisling*,
their nostalgia for the Stuart cause, but Ireland did not attempt to
rally either to the Old Pretender in 1715 or the young one in 1745.

Gaelic poetry flourished underground throughout the eighteenth
century and well into the nineteenth century, while Irish (Gaelic)
remained the vernacular of most of the people, as it did until the
great famine of the 1840s. The language, its literature and oral
traditions, kept alive the sense of identity of the suppressed people
and – together with the religious difference – fortified the tendency
to reject an alien government and social system. This had a revolutionary potential for the future, but its only outlets in the conditions
of the early and middle eighteenth century were agrarian. Both
revolution and open political organization were out of the question
in this period for the Gaelic Catholics: the defeats of the seventeenth century had been too crushing for anything but a very slow
recovery.

The active politics of Ireland during this period were Protestant
politics: the factor that was to begin the undoing of the conquest was
division among the conquerors. The maintenance and completion
of the conquest would have required the continuing unity and
reasonable harmony of three principal groups: the English government, the Irish parliament, and the most important body of settlers
in Ireland, the Presbyterians of Ulster. Had the English government consistently favoured the Ireland of the settlers, and had the
settlers themselves maintained a united front, the Gaelic and
Catholic element might perhaps have become a minority in modern
Ireland.

The Irish parliament was overwhelmingly Church of Ireland –
Anglican – in character, and the bishops of the Church of Ireland,
who were of course powerful in the House of Lords, were at this
time almost as hostile to Dissenters, including Presbyterians, as to
Roman Catholics. Swift's writings reflected this feeling: for him the
Catholics, detestable though their doctrines are, have been rendered
harmless; the present danger is inherent in dissent, the revolutionary
force from which his own family had suffered. A sacramental test
excluded Presbyterians, as well as Catholics, from civil and military employment. In practice, this was no extreme hardship, but it
had ominous implications: a large section of Protestants had now a
grievance in common with the Catholics.

English legislation and English governmental practice, by
operating against Irish interests – which in trade were mainly Protestant interests – caused the growth of a sense of Irish nationality:
for the settlers, at certain times, the sense of being Irish, as distinct

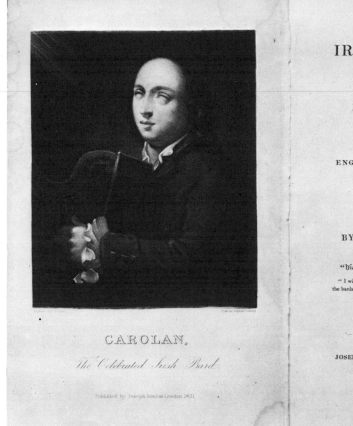

CAROLAN,

The Celebrated Irish Bard

Published by Joseph Robins London 1831

IRISH MINSTRELSY,

OR

BARDIC REMAINS OF IRELAND;

WITH

ENGLISH POETICAL TRANSLATIONS.

COLLECTED AND EDITED,

WITH NOTES AND ILLUSTRATIONS,

BY JAMES HARDIMAN, M. R. I. A.

"bíonn gráḋ agam ar ḋeantaiġh iʂ ar ceoltaiġh."

" I will give thee a book—it containeth the Songs of the bards of ERIN, of
the bards of the days that are gone." JOHN PHILPOT CURRAN.

VOL I.

LONDON:
JOSEPH ROBINS, BRIDE COURT, BRIDGE STREET.
1831.

from English, overshadowed that of being Protestant (of English origin) as distinct from Catholic (of Gaelic origin). English legislation, directed against Irish manufacture, helped to establish this sense of separate nationality.

One of the most promising branches of the Irish economy, and one of the first to recover from the devastation of the wars, was the woollen manufacture. As a result of the complaints of English manufacturers, the English parliament in 1699 ruined the Irish woollen industry, by prohibiting the export of woollen goods to any country except England, from which heavy duties in practice debarred them. The argument of William Molyneux (1656–98) that England had no constitutional right to legislate for Ireland was popular in Ireland, but condemned by the English parliament. The ruin of the woollen manufacture was not only damaging in itself – together with the Test Laws it helped to increase Presbyterian emigration to America – but it had ominous implications for industrial development in Ireland generally. Few would be prepared to

The publication of *Irish Minstrelsy* marked the revival of Catholic middle-class interest in the hidden Gaelic literature of the people, which had continued underground through centuries of proscription. The frontispiece shows the blind Irish harper, Carolan, who was much loved by all classes

81

A massive glass loving cup, typical of many pieces that kept Protestant feelings alive. It is engraved 'to the glorious and immortal memory of King William and his Queen Mary and perpetual disappointment to the Pope, the Pretender and all the enemies of the Protestant religion'

Opposite: Silver-gilt mace of the old Irish House of Lords, made in Dublin about 1766

invest in a country where success would be likely to attract penal legislation, through the influence of English competitors.

Irish Protestants became increasingly aware that the distinction between Protestant and Catholic, so basic in Ireland, was blurred in an English perspective. 'We seemed strange and remote to [the English],' wrote an Irish Protestant early in the eighteenth century, 'like a people setting up for ourselves. They looked on us as at a distance. . . . There was no one to explain the difference between the English and Irish inhabitants; and one impression [i.e. of all of them together] was that they were a disloyal and turbulent people, who could only be rendered harmless as long as they were disabled by poverty.'

Resentment against England reached its height among Irish Protestants when, in 1722, one William Wood, through influence with the King's mistress, obtained a patent, empowering him to coin money for Ireland. Against this transaction – about which no one in Ireland had been consulted – Swift wrote a series of powerful anonymous tracts: the *Drapier's Letters*. The fact that England and Ireland were under the same Crown did not, he argued, make Ireland dependent on England, or England superior to Ireland. 'Our neighbours whose understandings are just upon a level with ours (which perhaps are none of the brightest) have a strong contempt for most nations, but especially for Ireland.' Most important of all, Swift enunciated, as relevant to Ireland, a principle which was more far-reaching than he probably allowed for: 'All government without the consent of the governed is the very essence of slavery.'

Swift's tracts had an immense success with all classes in Ireland. 'The rage was universal', wrote the Lord-Lieutenant, Carteret. 'The Protestants having universally taken so unaccountable a turn, the Papists naturally followed suit to keep up the ferment.' The government gave way; Wood's patent was cancelled. Ireland was not, after all, quite as powerless as had seemed to be the case.

To the native Irish, the rifts between their conquerors allowed a gleam of hope. Yet the hope was equivocal. Could they really side either with the country that had conquered them, or with the settlers who held their lands? Some Catholics – and perhaps most of the clergy – seem to have thought that there was more hope of justice from an English government than from the Protestant Ascendancy in Ireland. This was to be the view of Edmund Burke, in his last years, and there can be little doubt that it represented one important, and rational, tradition among Catholics of the landed class, like Burke's Nagle relatives. But it is equally clear from the response to the Drapier – and from the affection which his name has inspired even to our own day – that defiance of England, even when it was

Henry Grattan: he stood for country rather than court

Protestant defiance, struck a deep answering chord in the Irish Catholic population generally. It is also clear, from Carteret's comment, that the existence of this response was among the factors which the English government had to take into account, and therefore among the levers of power available to the Irish Protestants – especially the middle class – in their disputes with England. Thus, the Irish Protestants had an incentive to relax the operation of the penal laws, while the English had an incentive to mitigate the system itself, in order to deprive Protestant discontent of potential Catholic allies. These factors worked rather slowly and intermittently, but they did begin, even in the first half of the eighteenth century, to disrupt the basis of the Protestant conquest.

By the 1760s a 'patriot' element – professing loyalty to the House of Hanover, but demanding greater autonomy for Ireland and generally also concessions to the Roman Catholics – had emerged in the Irish parliament. It was still a parliament largely managed on behalf of the English government, but the patriots, because of their popular support, were an influential minority. Their leaders were, first, Henry Flood (1732–91) and then, after Flood's defection, Henry Grattan (1746–1820). They found support among the Protestant middle class, especially the Presbyterians of the north, and among the Catholics generally. As trade was one of the few permitted outlets for Catholic activity, the Catholics now included a merchant interest, which shared with the Protestant middle class a desire to end the restrictions imposed by England on Irish trade. In this situation the old rigidity of religious antagonism weakened. 'Protestant' and 'Papist', a contemporary noted, had for the time ceased to be 'the key words'. It was now 'court' – meaning support for, and usually dependence on, the English government – or 'country', meaning the position of a 'patriot'.

The political alliance, in the patriot cause, of Protestants and Catholics – necessarily under Protestant leadership – was of its nature precarious. In the countryside the oppressed peasantry formed combinations for agrarian terrorism: the 'Whiteboys' and the 'Defenders'. Most Catholics, and people with strong Catholic connections, saw these movements as a legitimate response to the systematic injustice of the Irish land settlement. Even the ageing and conservative Edmund Burke was of this opinion: though the thought was 'odious' to him, he saw Catholic 'Defenderism' as 'the only restraint upon Protestant *ascendancy*'. Most Irish Protestants, even those of a decided patriotic turn, could not help seeing and feeling these matters differently. Even when they condemned, in the abstract, the injustices of the penal laws, and the oppressive conduct of many landlords, they were frightened by the hatred and desire for

revenge which lay behind defenderism. They were also made uneasy by the knowledge that their Catholic collaborators felt differently; they suspected that 'Catholic' and 'Defender' might mean
the same thing.

The correspondence of the poet and patriot William Drennan,
one of the founders of the United Irishmen (see p. 89), is illumi-
nating about this. Drennan was committed to Catholic emancipation, as well as to an Irish Republic, but neither he nor his like-
minded sister, Mrs McTier, was quite happy about the ultimate
implications of what they advocated. Drennan put to himself – after
some 'agrarian outrage' – the question of his opponents: 'Why
should we tolerate, why should we commit arms and rights to such
savages as these Catholics?' And he confessed that 'the only answer'
was, 'Why did you make them, and keep them savages, for that
they are such is without question.' He saw, he thought, 'as far into
the Catholic mind as others. I do not like it. It is a churlish soil, but
it is the soil of Ireland, and must be cultivated, or we must emigrate.'
And his sister, writing after the collapse of the movement for which
they had both risked so much, told of her feelings on hearing 'a

The Irish House of Commons.
A crowded House and gallery
listens to Henry Grattan
declaring that 'the people of
Ireland are of right an
independent nation', owing
allegiance to a common crown
but none to Westminster

Irish Volunteers in College Green, Dublin

Below: A badge presented by Lord Charlemont to the 1st Ulster Regiment of the Irish Volunteers, to be worn by the best shot in the regiment

singing procession' of Catholics: 'I begin to fear these people and think, like the Jews, they will regain their native land.'

The 1770s brought the first relaxation in the penal code, and concessions to Ireland generally. The outbreak of the American War of Independence made it expedient for the English govern-ment to appease public opinion in Ireland: Protestant and especially Presbyterian opinion was strongly pro-American. The war also provided a pretext for Protestant patriots to form an armed body, the Irish Volunteers; the ostensible object of this force was to defend Ireland's shores against foreign invasion, but it functioned in reality

as a lever to extort concessions from England. It was almost an exclusively Protestant body, but it enjoyed some Catholic support, and was, for a time, remarkably successful. It won, in 1780, the repeal of the laws forbidding the export of woollen and other goods; in 1782, the subordination of the Irish parliament to the English privy council was declared at an end, and Ireland was deemed to have acquired legislative independence, in the so-called 'Grattan's parliament' (1782–1800). The actual administration, however, remained in the hands of a Lord-Lieutenant, appointed by the English government.

Two of Dublin's finest buildings, the Law Courts (*above*) and the Custom House,
were built in the late eighteenth century, in a time of freer trade and rising prosperity

'Grattan's parliament', like contemporary parliaments in England, was an aristocratic body. It was faced with demands from the
Protestant middle class for parliamentary reform, and from the
Catholics for abolition of the penal laws. Parliament passed measures of Catholic relief but without, at first, conceding any political
power. It refused the Volunteers' demand for a great measure of
parliamentary reform. This was a period of considerable prosperity
for the landed and middle classes. The removal of restrictions on
trade benefited Dublin in particular, and several of the great buildings of the city – notably the Custom House, and the Four Courts –
date from this period. The condition of the peasantry was no less
miserable than before, and the Volunteers sometimes helped in the
suppression of agrarian disturbances.

Theobald Wolfe Tone

The impact of the French Revolution transformed the situation
in Ireland. The movement of the United Irishmen, in which the
leading spirit was Theobald Wolfe Tone (1763–98), sought to
make Ireland a republic on French principles, and to break the
connection with England. In the north of Ireland, as in industrial
England, a strong radical movement favoured the Revolution, and
there was wide support for the United Irishmen among the Presbyterians. Some Catholics also adhered to the movement, and Wolfe

The vote of a handsome cash
award to Henry Grattan from
the Irish House of Commons
inspired Gillray to a harshly
satirical cartoon

The arrest and mortal wounding of Lord Edward Fitzgerald. *Below:* this badge of the United Irishmen was taken from his body

Tone had considerable success in spreading his ideas in the countryside: 'Defenderism', from being purely an agrarian movement, became in many areas a revolutionary one. (This spread of French ideas was Yeats's 'Third Bell'.)

Burke urged that the best way of meeting the revolutionary threat was to make major concessions to the Catholics. Pitt began by moving in this direction. He used the influence which control of the Irish administration gave him over the Irish parliament to carry a major measure of Catholic emancipation, ending, in 1793, the refusal of the franchise to Catholics, though not ending their exclusion from parliament. Stiffening opposition from the Protestant Ascendancy prevented more far-reaching reforms. The recall of Lord Fitzwilliam in 1795 – after his attempt, as Lord-Lieutenant, to make conciliation of the Catholics the major object of his administration – was helpful to the revolutionary cause, as Burke saw with despair.

A French fleet, with Wolfe Tone aboard, sailed into Bantry Bay in December 1796, and although the French were prevented by bad weather from landing, their appearance encouraged the United

Irishmen. The government determined on a policy of repression – the alternation of conciliation and repression was to be the rhythm of English policy in Ireland for more than a century to come. Military coercion was applied first in Ulster in 1797, later in the rest of the country. In May 1798, after the arrest of many leading United Irishmen, and the capture and death of the popular hero, Lord Edward Fitzgerald (1763–98), rebellion broke out spasmodically and without a central plan. The main centres of the rebellion were in Ulster, where it was almost an entirely Protestant (Presbyterian) movement, and in Co. Wexford where, under the leadership of Father John Murphy, it was Catholic and took on some of the character of a religious war against Protestants. In both places the rebellion had been already put down, with great severity, when French help arrived in August 1798, in the west. The French were defeated and Wolfe Tone, captured aboard a French warship, was condemned to death. He died in prison, probably by his own hand.

Pitt, preoccupied with reducing the danger which Ireland presented to the security of England, had decided on a policy of legislative union, combined with full Catholic emancipation. Such a policy was in fact the logical conclusion to Burke's advice. As far as union was concerned, the condition of Ireland in the aftermath of

Killala Bay, in August 1798: French help arrived for the United Irishmen – too little, too late, and in the wrong place

Rebels of 1798 destroying a house and furniture: cartoon by Cruikshank

Opposite: At the head of Clew Bay, Co. Mayo, is Westport House, remodelled in the late eighteenth-century style by Thomas Ivory and James Wyatt

the rebellion was propitious, from Pitt's point of view. 'Grattan's Parliament' no longer had, for any large section of opinion, its old appeal. The unity which had made the strength of the Volunteer movement twenty years before was gone. Northern Presbyterians cared little for the parliament in College Green, and Catholic leaders favoured the Union, on the understanding that emancipation would follow. Key members of the landlord class, which had most to lose by the Union, were bought off by Castlereagh. On 28 March 1800, the terms of the Union were agreed by both Houses of the expiring Irish parliament, and on 1 January 1801 the United Kingdom of Great Britain and Ireland came into being.

Catholic emancipation was another matter. In Ireland, where the events of 1798, especially in Wexford, had reintensified religious animosities, there was strong Protestant opposition to any further measure of this kind. The Orange Order, founded in 1795 to combat defenderism and popery, had been hostile to the Union because of fears that it would be followed by emancipation. In England, not only was there a hostile movement of public opinion but George III himself set his face against the measure. Having won the Union, but failed to win emancipation, Pitt resigned in March 1801.

On 1 January 1801 the
United Kingdom of Great
Britain and Ireland came into
being, raising hopes of peace
and Catholic emancipation.
Gillray published this picture
of Anglo-Irish celebration.
Three months later, emancipation was abandoned, and Pitt
resigned

"We'll join in hand in hand, all Party shall cease,
"And Glass after Glass, shall our Union increase,

The execution of Robert Emmet in 1803

UNION-CLUB. { "In the cause of Old-England we'll drink down the Sun,
"Then toast Little Ireland, & drink down the Moon!"

Jan.ᵗ 21ˢᵗ 1801. by H Humphrey St James's Street.

CHAPTER 6

Catholic Resurgence and Protestant Reaction

The alignment of forces in Ireland after the Union resembled in some ways the alignment of the late seventeenth century, rather than that of the middle and later eighteenth century. The key words once again were 'Protestant' and 'Papist'. 'Grattan's Parliament' had abolished itself; of the patriot tradition among the Protestant landlord class, nothing was left except the memory of a few incorruptible men and a venal majority. The fragile unity of the United Irishmen was gone too. The Presbyterians, as a body, ceased to have any revolutionary inclinations: they became pillars of the Union, and of the Orange Order. Tone's principles, abandoned by those who had first welcomed them, became an important intellectual ferment in the Catholic population.

To those who regarded themselves as Tone's heirs – and these included the men of 1916, and many of those who led the revolutionary struggle from 1918 on – the defection of the Presbyterians came to seem mysterious and unnatural. It has been explained by deliberate governmental exploitation of religious differences. This did take place, but it is doubtful whether it could have had much success, had it not been favoured by profound historical and psychological factors. An alliance of settlers and dispossessed natives was necessarily a precarious affair, and lacked – as we can see from the Drennan letters – any great cordiality. News like that of Wexford, and of the brief rising of Robert Emmet (1778–1803) in Dublin in 1803, was bound to frighten people who, on grounds of abstract principle and general policy, and contrary to their own traditions and early prejudices, had sought to ally themselves with the suppressed majority which now seemed to intend their destruction. Protestants began to see dependence on England not as the odious thing it had seemed to the self-confident patriots of the eighteenth century, but as the best guarantee for their own lives and

Robert Emmet, leader of a short-lived revolt soon after the Union

liberties, threatened by a revengeful Catholic *jacquerie*. The reactionary movement which swept through Great Britain at this period certainly encouraged these sentiments, but did not create them. The decisive event had probably been Wolfe Tone's success in disseminating revolutionary ideas among the peasantry. Once the consequences were understood, this dissemination was bound to discourage the middle-class radicals who had been the core of the United Irishmen. For this group the representative voice was to become that of Mrs McTier: 'I begin to fear these people.'

The lines harden

The Catholics, whose leaders had originally favoured union, naturally felt betrayed when the promised emancipation did not follow. The lines, which had been shifting for so long, soon became clear and hard again. 'Protestant' and 'Unionist' were to become virtually synonymous. Catholic rejection of the Union was to have various names, associated with different methods towards essentially the same end: 'Repeal', 'Home Rule', 'Sinn Fein'. For the Catho-

lics, the Protestants were no longer champions of 'the Irish nation' containing, in however shadowy a form, an ideal of unity and freedom. They had become again, with few but noticeable exceptions, certainly by 1820, what they had been in 1690: England's garrison in Ireland. Yet the memory of the intervening years had its potency. The 'common name of Irishman' – Wolfe Tone's device – the words of Swift, Molyneux and Grattan, the words and actions of Tone and Emmet, had entered the imagination of the people of Ireland. The struggle could no longer be seen in terms of a war of religion. It would be a struggle of national liberation, the vocabulary of which was acquired by the conquered, mainly from children of the conquerors. Trinity College, Queen Elizabeth's foundation, was at last beginning to reach the people, though not in the sense that had been intended. Swift, Molyneux, Grattan, Tone and Emmet all had studied there, and through them the concept of Irish nationality took form.

Trinity College, Dublin:
watercolour by James Malton,
1790

A DANIEL—A DANIEL COME TO JUDGMENT!

Daniel O'Connell, leader of the Catholic emancipation movement, built up a mass movement on the basis of a penny a month subscription – the 'Catholic rent'. This was an irresistible target for *Punch*'s humour

The first phase of the struggle of the submerged people was that of a demand for political equality which had been denied by a religious test. Superficially the demand for 'emancipation' – the right of Catholics to sit in parliament – might have seemed to be a diversion from the real issues. In the unreformed parliament of the United Kingdom few Catholics would be elected and even after reform they would always be in a minority: emancipation in itself could bring no cure to Ireland's social and economic distress. Yet it was of critical importance in several ways.

Symbolically, it marked the end of the penal system, the return to existence of people whom the law had presumed not to exist. It weakened the position of 'the garrison' by ending the Protestant monopoly of parliamentary representation. As it happened, by far

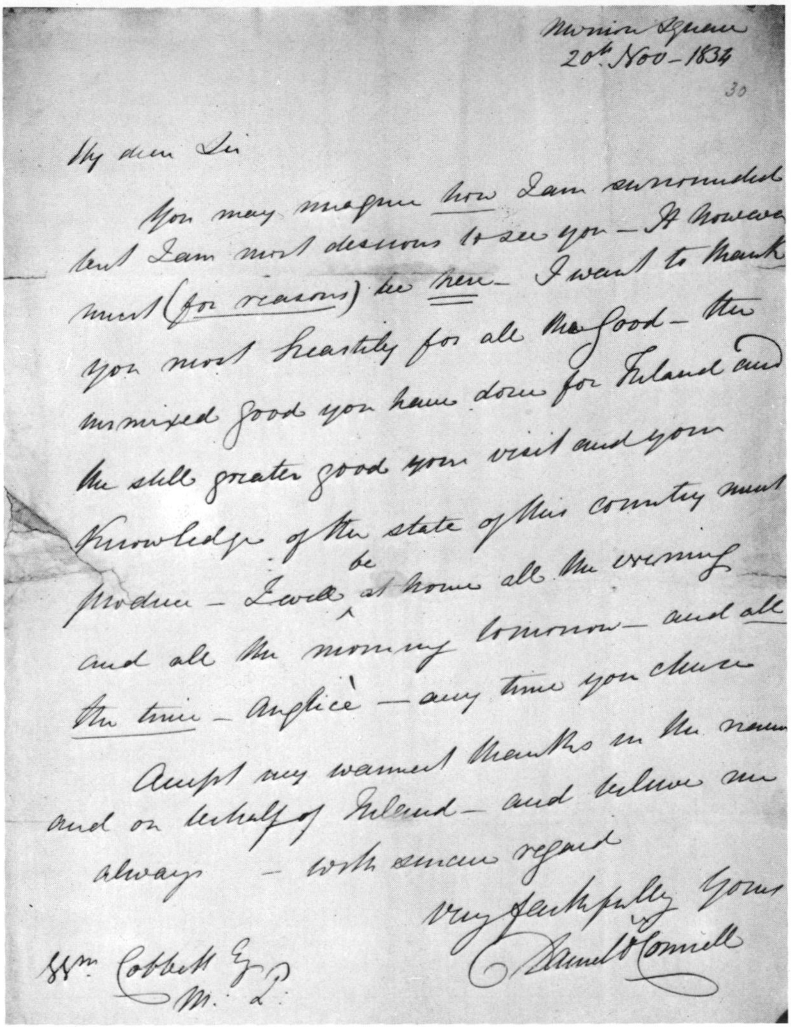

My dear Sir

You may imagine how I am surrounded but I am most desirous to see you — It however must (for reasons) be here — I want to thank you most heartily for all the good — the unmixed good you have done for Ireland and the still greater good your visit and your knowledge of the state of this country must produce — I will be at home all the evening — and all the morning tomorrow — and all the time — Anglicé — any time you chuse

Accept my warmest thanks in the name and on behalf of Ireland — and believe me always — with sincere regard

Very faithfully Yours
Daniel O'Connell

Merrion Square
20ᵗʰ Nov — 1834

Wm. Cobbett Esq.
M. P.

William Cobbett, English radical M.P. and journalist, gave valuable support to the cause of Catholic emancipation and reform, as Daniel O'Connell gratefully recognizes in this letter

the most effective parliamentary leader of the Catholic people was to be a Protestant, Charles Stewart Parnell (1845–91), but the party which he led, and which constituted his political force, could not have come into being without emancipation, and the subsequent widening of the franchise. And this parliamentary party was to prove an essential prong for the attack on the Irish land system and the basis of the conquest.

The process of winning emancipation was not less important than emancipation itself. Under a leader of immense energy and resource, Daniel O'Connell (1775–1847), the first political mass movement of the Irish people was brought into being. The great engine of the agitation was the institution, from 1824, of the 'Catholic rent', which allowed a mass membership to O'Connell's Catholic

Daniel O'Connell

Thomas Davis, intellectual leader of the 'Young Ireland' nationalists

Association, by admitting members for a fee of a penny a month. On this basis, and through O'Connell's extraordinary command over great crowds, one of the most effective of modern political mass movements was called into being. O'Connell's own election for Clare, in 1828, his subsequent exclusion from parliament, and address from the bar of the House, dramatized the Catholic situation, and made a certain impact on English public opinion. Catholic emancipation became a reality in 1829.

It is sometimes suggested that if Catholic emancipation had been conceded simultaneously with the passage of the Act of Union, Catholic gratitude to England might have made the Union permanent. This hardly seems likely: the resentments created by several centuries of subjugation, and one of legal degradation, could hardly be obliterated by a statute. But the fact of having to win emancipation, instead of merely having it accorded, probably did something to create confidence in the possibilities of political action: without this, it is conceivable that most of the Catholic people might have resigned themselves to the Union, as something beyond their power to change.

The Catholics were now to experience the limitations, as well as the possibilities, of mass agitation. The 'monster meetings', through which O'Connell conducted his agitation for the repeal of the Union, were successful as demonstrations of popular support, but ended in fiasco. O'Connell cancelled what was intended to be the climactic meeting, at Clontarf, in October 1843, when it was proscribed by the government. This 'surrender' strengthened the determination of the more 'extreme' nationalists of Young Ireland, a body formed by a graduate of Trinity College, Thomas Davis (1814–45), on the principles of an uncompromising and defiant Irish nationalism, and veneration of the heroes of past insurrections, especially that of 1798. The teaching of this school pointed clearly to rebellion, which broke out in 1848, under the chivalrous and incompetent leadership of William Smith O'Brien (1803–64). The rising was easily put down, and it seemed as if Young Ireland's road to independence was as impracticable as O'Connell's. But in fact 1848 helped to establish the continuity of a revolutionary tradition; those who were to lead the rising of 1916 were lineal successors of the men of 1848: key figures among these 1916 men belonged to the Irish Republican Brotherhood, founded by James Stephens (1824–1901), one of the most determined of the 1848 rebels.

In the Ireland of 1848, however, a rebellion could only be a gesture, and a pledge for the future. The Ireland of that time was an Ireland devastated by the great famine, produced by the failure of the potato crop in 1845, 1846 and 1847. The population of Ireland

had, up to this time, been very rapidly increasing; from about five million at the time of the Union to over eight million in 1841. It was a rate of increase almost comparable with that which is occurring in tropical countries in our own time, and it took place in similar conditions, of subsistence agriculture – the staple diet of the Irish being the potato – rural overcrowding and miserable conditions of life. Since Ireland lacks coal and iron, and its history had not been conducive to the growth of special skills, industrious habits, or conditions attractive to investors, the Industrial Revolution which was transforming the neighbouring land had largely passed Ireland by, except for the north-east, where the Protestant population, increasingly re-emphasizing its difference from the rest of the country, was developing linen and shipbuilding industries. For the expanding population of the rest of the country there was no outlet, once the limit of cultivation had been reached, or in the event of a failure of a crop, except in emigration or death. In the great famine it is estimated that a million emigrated – mainly to the United

Female labour in an Ulster flax-mill. The Industrial Revolution came late to Ireland

A rising population, followed by famine,
led to large-scale emigration from Ireland
to America in the 1840s and 1850s.
Right: a conventionally tatterdemalion
Mick studies the sailings, and *(below)*
Samuel B. Waugh's painting *The
Battery, New York* (about 1855) shows
the end of the journey

States – and a million died. Emigration continued on a great scale thereafter, and the population of the whole country today is about half what it was before the famine.

In Ireland – and above all among Americans of Irish origin, most of whom are descended from famine emigrants – popular tradition regards the famine as 'man-made', in the sense that England was glad to be rid of the Irish and did nothing, or very little, to check the ravages of the disaster. 'Thou shalt not kill; but needst not strive Officiously to keep alive.' Contemporary English opinion generally inclined to think of the disaster as one which had come on the Irish as a result of their own thriftless and improvident way of life: 'famine', as Spenser had written on an earlier occasion, 'which they themselves had wrought'.

Historians, both English and Irish, generally see the outbreak of famine as inevitable, but think that disaster on the scale which actually occurred could have been avoided by more determined governmental action. Some of them see the root cause of the failure to take such action as lying in the economic theory of the time: the doctrines of the Manchester school, forbidding state interference with the working of economic laws. This may be so: we cannot know whether the English government would have been equally faithful

The potato famine of 1846. A contemporary engraving shows a starving crowd at the gate of a workhouse

The great famine

to the Manchester school had famine broken out in, say, Manchester. It is possible that they would: governments and economists of the period were inclined to regard the sufferings of the poor, of whatever nationality, as part of the natural order of things. But it is also true that English governments had never interested themselves energetically in the affairs of Ireland, except when these presented, or seemed to present, a threat to the security of England. The famine did not seem to present such a threat: rather it must have seemed to reduce a threat which had long existed, in the presence and growth of a population known to be animated by inveterate hostility towards England. Granted all this, the lack of urgency in the English government's approach to the problem has nothing mysterious about it. Some individual Englishmen, and groups of Englishmen and Irishmen – notably the Society of Friends – did all that they could to mitigate the effects of the tragedy, but help on the great scale which alone would have sufficed to avert it was not forthcoming.

The famine is the great dividing line in modern Irish history. Before it, Ireland had been a country of notably early marriages; after it, late marriages are the rule, and the most conspicuous social feature of contemporary Ireland. The only method of birth control practicable in Catholic Ireland was being applied. There was a change in language also. Before the famine Ireland was to a great extent Irish speaking; after it, English was soon spoken almost everywhere, except in some parts of the western seaboard. One may also feel that there was a certain change in the character of the people. The picture of a happy-go-lucky Irishman may well have been partly mythical – like its Negro equivalent – but seems to contain some truth for, say, the contemporaries of O'Connell. After the famine one senses a new quality, something grimmer and tougher, among the survivors and their children, the Irish of the later nineteenth century.

Ireland and America   The political consequences of this were not to be felt in full for another generation: until the children who experienced the famine and immediate post-famine years had reached maturity, in Ireland and in America. The great new factor in Irish politics was to be the growth of this Irish community in America – for a long time it remained more Irish than American. Poor as it remained by American standards, by Irish standards it was soon rich, and it was generous in support of any movement for Irish independence that looked at all promising. This new factor was to bring about a great weakening of England's control over Ireland. From now on, as an English Home Secretary was to complain in the stormy 1880s, an important section of the perennially rebellious Irish nation was 'out of reach'.

With the increase of the relative importance of America in world politics, the Irish in America, with their well-organized voting strength, could begin to apply pressure on Britain through their own government. By the 1920s, the government of Lloyd George could no more afford to ignore the Irish of New York, in relation to implementation of its policy in Ireland, than Ernest Bevin at a later date could ignore the reaction of the Jews of New York to his policy in Palestine.

The famine may not have been a threat to the security of England, but it carried within itself the seeds of the destruction of the United Kingdom of Great Britain and Ireland.

In the confused and often seemingly pointless politics of the period immediately following the famine and the death of O'Connell, the most purposeful and creative figure is that of James Stephens, 'the Fenian Chief'. Stephens's 'Funeral' took place in Kilkenny in 1848; it was in fact a successful diversion and the ingenious rebel escaped, unpunished, to France. His principles were those of Wolfe Tone and he devoted his life to conspiracy for the attainment of Tone's objectives. His organization, from 1858 on,

A St Patrick's Day parade in Union Square, New York, in the 1870s. The Irish-American community was becoming an important force in Irish politics

The Fenians

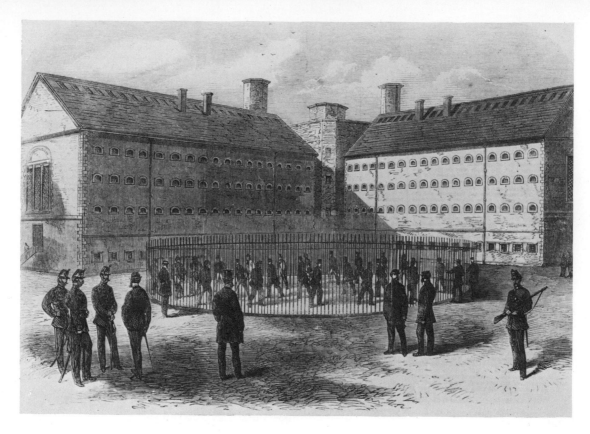

Mountjoy Prison, Dublin, in the 1860s. Here were imprisoned many of the Fenian conspirators

had two branches: the Irish Republican Brotherhood, in Ireland itself, and the Fenian Brotherhood (later Clan na Gael) in America. These revolutionary bodies soon escaped from Stephens's autocratic control, but they continued, up to the achievement of independence, to be important, partly hidden elements in Irish politics. Militarily, they produced little result in the time of their founder. The 'Fenian risings' of 1865 and 1867 were not very much more dangerous than that of 1848: there were men of military experience connected with these risings – veterans of the American Civil War – but they did not know Irish conditions, and overruled Stephens, who did. The two societies remained, however, of importance as a continuing conspiracy involving a number of men of remarkable determination, and some political minds of high order. They constituted, for the younger members, a school of revolution.

Out of the Fenian movement, and the experience of defeat and imprisonment, came a new and entirely original political concept: the combination of revolutionary conspiracy and open agrarian agitation with parliamentary action. The moving spirits in the 'New Departure' – as this combination was justifiably called – were John Devoy (1842–1928) in America and Michael Davitt

(1846–1906) in Ireland. Both men had served sentences of penal servitude for their part in the Fenian movement. Davitt – whose father had been evicted from his Mayo farm in the wake of the famine – had lost his right arm in a Lancashire mill at the age of eleven. Both men remained determined to achieve the Fenian objectives but they were not, as some of their comrades were, confined by any doctrinaire objection to 'open' or 'constitutional' methods. The main, and formidable, instrument of the New Departure was the Land League, founded on Davitt's initiative in 1878–9.

In the Land League, Fenian determination and organizing drive connected with the deep discontent of the people on the land to produce a popular movement, comparable in scale to that of O'Connell's day, but relying no longer solely on agitation. The Land League used a mixture of O'Connell's methods – mass meetings, brass bands and tar-barrels – with quieter forms of social combination and pressure. Its policy was to select estates especially notorious for rack-renting and eviction; concentrate public attention on these estates, by means of mass meetings; and then, by pressure of social ostracism and refusal of services, render life as difficult as possible for the landlord (if resident) or his agent, and especially

Michael Davitt, whose Land League derived from the Fenian Brotherhood and peasant discontent for 'grabbers' – those who rented land from which the previous tenants had been evicted, and which the Land League had placed under ban. The spectacular application of these methods in 1880 against a Mayo estate, for which a certain Captain Boycott was agent, gave the word 'boycott' to the English language, and to many other languages.

The years 1878–81, in which the Land League took hold, were years of great agricultural distress: many feared a repetition of the great famine. In the popular response to the Land League there was something of the courage of despair, and something of shame at the unresisting manner in which so many of the generation of the forties had gone to their death. In some ways the feelings of the dour gener‑ation of Irishmen that broke the landlord power are comparable to those of post‑holocaust Jews. In both cases, after great disasters, previous national stereotypes were rejected, and a change of tone and temperament took place. The boycott was no more 'feckless' or 'happy‑go‑lucky' than the State of Israel was lacking in combative‑ness. And part of the effectiveness of the New Departure, as of the Zionists, lay in the way in which the efforts of those at home were sustained by the money of the diaspora.

The success of the Land League, which was undeniable, was ascribed by its enemies to a combination of American money – 'the pennies of the Irish servant‑girls' – and intimidation. The role of the American money could hardly be denied: the Land League as a national organization, with a small, ingenious and hard‑working bureaucracy of its own, could hardly have been sustained, in the conditions of the time, without this aid. Intimidation was denied and sometimes, in its more violent forms, actually discouraged by Land League leaders. But there can be little doubt that intimida‑tion – whether deplored or condoned by the leadership – was a significant element in the social reality of the Land League move‑ment. The Land League was a vastly more efficient and intelligently conducted engine of agrarian change than the old secret societies, Whiteboys, Defenders, Ribbonmen and the rest, but it had exactly the same social origins – Michael Davitt's father had headed an agrarian secret society in Mayo – and never entirely abjured in practice the use, or at least the threat, of the old methods. When John Dillon suggested that 'two active young men' in every parish should visit any farmer who held out against the Land League, he clearly envisaged a persuasion which ultimately would not rely ex‑clusively on rhetoric. But what those who emphasized intimidation usually overlooked, or ignored, was that the Land League would have had no power to intimidate dissidents had it not possessed overwhelming popular support. The landlords, backed by the full

The Land League was a formidable and well-organized instrument against rack-renting and evictions (*top*), which were supported by magistrates and police (*centre*). The picture below, obviously sympathetic to the landlords, talks of 'wire-pullers' and 'puppets', but the Land League's strength was in its mass support

Charles Stewart Parnell,
Protestant leader of a Catholic
peasantry

Parnell

apparatus of state power, had relied for centuries on coercion and the threat of coercion, and their insistence that their enemies should depend entirely on pacific methods was not convincing, either in England or in Ireland.

Just as Tone had sought, through spreading his revolutionary principles among the agrarian Defenders, to achieve not only social change but also his political objective of breaking the connection with England, so the initiators of the New Departure sought to begin a political revolution with a social one. In a sense they succeeded, but not in their own time. They envisaged that the political stage of the revolution should begin by the withdrawal from parliament of the 'active section' of the Irish parliamentary representation, which professed Land League principles. This idea of secession was revived, in the following century, by Sinn Fein, with powerful effect. That was after several decades of parliamentary activity, after the executions of 1916 and in a world situation transformed by the First World War. The conditions of the seventies and eighties were not so propitious, and the founders of the New Departure never seem to have clearly envisaged just what would, or could, follow the secession of the parliamentarians. The result might well have been another Clontarf.

In any case the decision was not to be taken by the political strategists who devised the New Departure, but by an unrivalled master of political tactics, who was first their ally and then leader of the movement which they had begun. Charles Stewart Parnell was an Irish landlord, elected for Meath in 1875, who had attracted considerable attention by his intransigent nationalism even before the New Departure, and who attracted much more after he emerged as the chief parliamentary champion of the Land League cause. The assumption by a Protestant landlord of the leadership of the whole Catholic peasantry was generally regarded as paradoxical, and was in fact unprecedented. There were, however, elements in Parnell's background which distinguished him from most of his class. His great-grandfather, Sir John Parnell, had been among the 'incorruptibles' who voted against the Union; it was not inconsistent that Sir John's descendant should seek to disrupt it. More important, probably, was the influence of his American mother, whose father, Commodore Charles Stewart, had fought against England in the War of 1812. The Stewarts had emigrated to America from Belfast in the period just before the American Revolution, and it seems that the family tradition included some of the anti-English tone which had characterized much of the north of Ireland in the eighteenth century.

Parnell was, in 1879, a more conspicuous figure than Davitt – or, of course, the distant Devoy – both socially and politically; the unpopularity in England and among his own class which followed his adoption of Land League principles – seen as a betrayal of his kind – automatically increased his popularity and his conspicuousness in Catholic Ireland. The return in the general elections of 1880, through Land League support, of a number of new and more radical Irish members led to the election of Parnell as chairman of the Irish parliamentary party; since 1877 he had been chairman of the Home Rule Confederation of Great Britain, and his followers soon began to refer to him as leader of the Irish people at home and abroad. Ably, he continued to press home the great land agitation, but avoided secession, or any attempt at political revolution.

The movement won a great success when, in 1881, Gladstone carried through a Land Act, conceding a number of principles which the tenants had long been demanding: notably legal assessment of 'fair rents' and security against arbitrary eviction. This Act transformed the conditions of land tenure in Ireland, and cracked the entire basis of the Cromwellian settlement; once the landlords' authority became conditional and open to question it was only a

Kilmainham Jail, where Parnell and other Irish leaders were imprisoned

Artist's impression of the Phoenix Park murders. Mr Burke lies dead on the grass; Lord Frederick Cavendish faces the terrorists

matter of time, as both landlords and tenants saw, before it would cease to exist.

This triumph for the Land League – as it stands out in retrospect – was not, and could not be, enough for those to whom the agrarian agitation was only a means to political revolution. In a sense Parnell shared their purpose – but only if by 'revolution' we mean the greatest degree of independence practically obtainable. He had no intention of leading an armed rebellion, which he judged impracticable, but neither did he intend to allow himself to be classed with his parliamentary predecessor, Isaac Butt, as one who had come to terms with England and deserted the national cause. In the circumstances, by a classical political detour, he adopted the style and tone of those whose policy he had really rejected. This provocative language led, as no doubt he intended, to his imprisonment: Kilmainham Jail was undoubtedly the most desirable residence, politically speaking, for an Irish leader at this time.

Under the leadership of the extreme wing the land agitation continued in spasmodic violence, but everywhere the tenants, who clearly saw the value of the Land Act, were taking advantage of it. It was now possible to reshape the whole movement, in the sense of Parnell's intention, which was not the same as Davitt's. Parnell came to terms with Gladstone, which led to his release in May 1882.

It is possible that this 'Kilmainham treaty' might have seriously injured Parnell's authority with the Irish majority – as it certainly did with 'extremists' like his own sisters – had it not been for the shock administered by the Phoenix Park murders: the assassination, by a group of political terrorists, of the Chief Secretary for Ireland, Lord Frederick Cavendish, and the Under-Secretary, T.H. Burke. As it was, Parnell was not only not seriously attacked: but he was able, without any notable opposition, to reorganize the structure of what had been the Land League.

The new body which was now founded, the National League, was firmly under parliamentarian control, with the full co-operation, in a 'constitutional nationalist' spirit, of the Catholic clergy. The National League retained enough of its Land League impetus and following to be an effective popular organization. Its main purpose was now to provide an electoral machine for Parnell's party. In this it was highly successful. At the next general elections, those of 1885, Parnell's followers became the whole of the Irish representation, outside the Protestant north-east and the representation of Trinity College. With a following of eighty-five pledge-bound members, Parnell held the balance of power in the House of Commons.

A. J. Balfour, Chief Secretary for Ireland, portrayed in a contemporary cartoon as a defeated bully, offers Ireland her own autonomous university if she will abandon her own Parliament. Parnell assures him that Ireland means to have both, 'and no thanks to you for either'

Balfour, architect of the coercion policy, caricatured by Frank Carruthers Gould in the *Pall Mall Gazette*

Gladstone and Home Rule

Opposite: Britannia stands at the cross-roads, offered conflicting advice. Is she to heed Gladstone the Liberal, holding the olive branch of Home Rule, or the Conservative Lord Salisbury with nothing to offer but coercion?

It was in these conditions that Gladstone decided to introduce a Bill granting Home Rule to Ireland. His enemies, naturally, saw this as a bid to hold office at any price. Gladstone, however, had long cherished a desire to bring about a fundamental, reconciling change in the relations between England and Ireland. The new situation, and the clear Home Rule mandate of the Irish electorate, seemed to bring a Home Rule attempt within the range of practical politics. The attempt was more than many of his followers, and most of the English electorate, could tolerate at this time. Under Joseph Chamberlain, then in transit from radicalism to imperialism, a section of the Liberals broke away, and with the Tories, defeated the Home Rule Bill. At the subsequent elections the Tories came back into office, with coercion as their immediate policy for Ireland.

Gladstone's defeat need not have been decisive; many reasonably assumed that it was not. The resumption of the agrarian struggle, under the ingenious rent-funding forms of the 'Plan of Campaign' (1887), proved that Tory coercion was not necessarily a panacea for Irish unrest. Co-operation – originally hesitant – between Gladstone Liberals and Irish Home Rulers grew warmer and more effective as the end of the decade approached. Gladstone attained, in Ireland, a popularity never even remotely approached by any other English statesman before or since. The 'union of hearts' – the phrase dear to Liberal and Irish orators at this time – was probably never as complete as Home Rulers liked to say it was, but there was certainly a shift in Irish opinion: for most people the enemy, at this time, was

Katharine O'Shea – the diminutive 'Kitty' was bestowed by Parnell's enemies

no longer 'the English' but a section of them: the Tories and – especially – Chamberlain.

English opinion showed in general no corresponding warming to Parnell until, in 1889, it was proved that charges made against him by *The Times* – of having condoned the Phoenix Park murders – rested on forgeries. This helped to discredit the Tories generally and – more particularly – the picture of Ireland and the Home Rule movement which the Tories had presented. Gladstone's moral authority was enhanced, and Parnell ceased to seem a dubious and discreditable ally. By the end of 1889, the conjuncture looked extremely favourable to Home Rule. It looked as if the next elections should bring Gladstone a large majority and a mandate so clear that the Lords would offer no resistance. Contemporaries tended to assume that, granted a clear majority in the United Kingdom parliament in favour of Home Rule, the Protestants of Ulster would offer no resistance. In fact, Ulster Protestants, alarmed by the threat of becoming a minority in a Catholic-dominated Home Rule Ireland, were rallying to the Orange Order in increasing numbers, and already considering armed resistance.

In 1890, however, a personal and political tragedy upset all calculations. Captain W. H. O'Shea, formerly member of parliament for an Irish constituency and an associate of Joseph Chamberlain's, took divorce proceedings against his wife, Katharine, citing Parnell as co-respondent. When the divorce suit was undefended it was at first assumed that Parnell would resign. This assumption, while reasonable according to prevailing conventions, was wrong. The Irish party, accustomed to give Parnell unquestioning obedience, reacted in confusion. They re-elected him as chairman and then – after Gladstone, responding to English Nonconformist opinion on the matter, came out against him – the majority of the party declared their chairman deposed. They were supported by the Catholic hierarchy, which is hardly surprising, and later by the bulk of the electorate. He fought and lost three bitter by-elections and died at Brighton on 6 October 1891.

Parnell's movement had won a radical measure of land reform: it had also broken the solidity, in England, of the prevalent assumption that no special political status could be accorded to Ireland. These were Parnell's main achievements up to 1890. In 1890–91, however, his achievements were of a different kind. He appealed to the revolutionary tradition which in his heyday he had restrained. The Fenians supported him, and his stature, and romantic fall, helped to give the Fenians, and not the constitutional parliamentarians, authority with the young. He praised, and summoned back to Ireland, James Stephens. The Fenian chief arrived in time to lay

a wreath of immortelles on Parnell's grave. It was he, and not any one of Parnell's constitutional followers, who was elected to succeed Parnell as patron of the Cork branch of the Gaelic Athletic Association. Tim Healy, Parnell's most bitter assailant, had not been impressed by the victory of himself and his, quite temporary, friends. 'We have the voters,' he wrote, 'but Parnell has their sons.' It might have been equally true to say that Parnell had given their sons to James Stephens.

This was the Fourth Bell. 'The modern literature of Ireland,' Yeats told the Swedish Academy in 1923, 'and indeed all that stir of thought which prepared for the Anglo-Irish war, began when Parnell fell from power in 1891. A disillusioned and embittered Ireland turned from parliamentary politics; an event was conceived, and a race began, as I think, to be troubled by that event's long gestation.'

Tenniel's cartoon in *Punch* shows Tim Healy (in glasses) and Parnell battling it out as the two villains in *The Babes in the Wood*, while the babes, Gladstone and Ireland, look nervously on

The port of Dublin in the 1880s, looking down the Liffey from the Custom House

Three great literary figures: James Joyce (*above, left*),
W.B. Yeats (*left*) and J.M. Synge

CHAPTER 7

The Struggle for Independence

Shame at the passivity or treachery of an earlier generation has been a powerful motive force in modern Irish history. The Land League generation felt in this way about the sheep-to-the-slaughter generation of the great famine. And the Land League generation – the generation of Parnell's contemporaries – were themselves to appear to their successors as traitors or cowards: the men who had thrown Parnell to the wolves at the bidding of an Englishman. W.B. Yeats, who was twenty-five at the time of the fall of Parnell, wrote immediately a patriotic elegy, *Mourn and then Onwards*, and returned to the theme years afterwards in *Parnell's Funeral*:

> An age is the reversal of an age:
> When strangers murdered Emmet, Fitzgerald, Tone,
> We lived like men that watch a painted stage.
> What matter for the scene, the scene once gone;
> It had not touched our lives. But popular rage,
> *Hysterica passio* dragged this quarry down.
> None shared our guilt: nor did we play a part
> Upon a painted stage when we devoured his heart.

James Joyce, who was nine at the time, wrote as his first imaginative work *Et tu Healy*! – a play against Parnell's most scurrilous adversary – and also returned to the theme in his maturity, both in *Dubliners* ('Ivy Day in the Committee Room') and in a famous scene in *A Portrait of the Artist as a Young Man*:

O he'll remember all this when he grows up, said Dante hotly – the language he heard against God and religion and priests in his own home. – Let him remember too, cried Mrs Casey to her from across the table, the language with which the priests and the priests' pawns broke Parnell's heart and hounded him into his grave. Let him remember that too when he grows up.

The fall of Parnell opened a double crisis of authority inside Irish Society. Parental authority was shaken, and so – in some ways more

gravely – was the authority of the Catholic clergy. The priests had carried with them through the nineteenth century the moral authority which the faith of the people, the steadfastness of earlier priests under long persecution, and the lack of other educated leaders in the poorer parts of the country conferred on them. This moral authority was not destroyed by the Parnell crisis, and for most people it was not even weakened in a fundamental sense, but its sphere became more narrowly defined; the idea that politics lay outside this sphere became dominant, precisely among those Irish-men who were most passionately interested in politics.

The idea of keeping religion out of politics was not, of course, new. Ever since Tone's efforts to disseminate French Revolutionary ideas in Ireland, there had been a tension in the Irish mind between Catholicism and nationalism. The principal Irish Catholic semi-nary, St Patrick's Royal College, Maynooth, had been founded in 1795 under the influence of Edmund Burke: its founders certainly had in mind the Burkian concept of Catholicism as a bulwark against Jacobinism. The Irish Republicanism of Wolfe Tone's followers was identified as a form of Jacobinism. The influence of the Vatican, a counter-revolutionary force in nineteenth-century Europe, was used, normally with discretion, in support of English rule in Ireland.

Yet in Ireland itself the opposition between 'clerical counter-revolutionaries' and 'Jacobins' had not been nearly as strong in reality as the terms would imply. The 'Jacobins' were seldom militantly hostile to religion, though they were often uneasy about it: many of the clergy, including perhaps a majority of the junior clergy, were much more nationalist than the founders of Maynooth, or the Popes, would have liked. They laid stress on the hopelessness of rebellion – and the theological principle that its hopelessness made it immoral – rather than on the legitimacy of constituted authority. The mass of the people tended to 'obey the priests' – about not taking part in hopeless risings like those of 1849 and 1865 – but also to venerate, virtually as martyrs, those who, disobeying such admonitions, lost their lives in such rebellions.

The higher clergy initially opposed the Land League agitation, both because the condemned 'Fenians' were involved in it, and out of general principles of social conservativism. The argument of 'hopelessness' was not, however, available against this powerful movement, and the advice of bishops, and even of the Pope at a later stage, had little effect. The idea of 'no priests in politics' gained some ground, but the priests returned to politics, 'on the right centre of the army of agitation', as was said at the time, and as part of the Parnell movement. Parnell needed the priests from 1882 on,

Opposite: St Patrick's Royal College, Maynooth, the principal Catholic seminary of Ireland

Hunting scene by Œnone Somerville. In her best-known books, those she wrote with 'Martin Ross', the Irish were charming and humorous stereotypes, not to be taken seriously

because he was breaking with the Fenians in order to follow a constitutional course.

In 1890 the divorce case – an accident from a political point of view – necessarily cost him the support of the priests and he turned to the Fenians again. The priests were committed to his political destruction, but insisted that they were not pursuing a political end. They were telling the truth, but their very insistence on the primacy of a point of sexual morality, and the puritanical violence of some of their language, made them appear in a repulsive light to many of the young. Their own self-confidence may also have been shaken; more than thirty years were to elapse, and much blood was to be

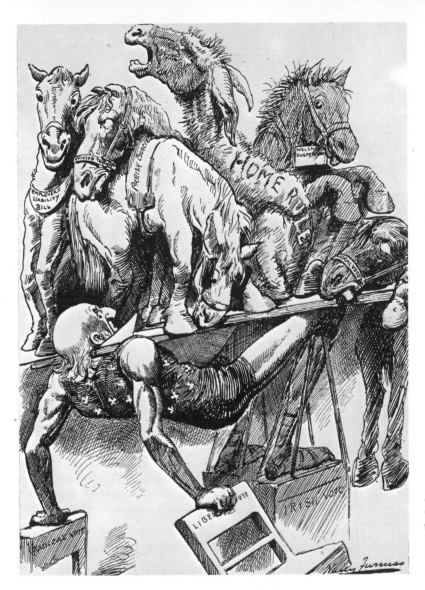

Even the Grand Old Man could only bear so much, as this *Punch* cartoon suggests. His second Home Rule Bill was thrown out by the House of Lords in 1893

shed, before they again took as vigorous or united a stand on any issue affecting politics as they had taken in 1891.

The Fenian doctrine – revolutionary, anti-clerical and derived from Tone – had hitherto reached only a rather small section of the young: on the fall of Parnell it reached large numbers of young people, who had been brought up almost to worship Parnell, and who were profoundly shocked by being suddenly invited to treat him with contempt. Several kinds of rebellion and rejection now fused. Sean O'Faolain, who was not born at the time of Parnell's fall, but who grew up among its sullen and protracted echoes, has the central character of his second novel *Bird Alone* (1936) find

The Gaelic League was founded in 1893 to keep the Irish language alive and to preserve Irish customs and dress – generally to foster the independent Irish identity. *Above:* Lord Ashbourne, the League's President, wears the Irish kilt. The painting, about 1915, is by Clare Marsh

justification, from the misery and frustration of his personal life, in the Parnellite image of the hero betrayed by priests: 'what had happened to me was an image of the far worse that had happened to...the Fenians, to the Land Leaguers, to Parnell'.

We cannot know how widespread such feelings were; we know that they were intense and affected an intelligent, creative and active minority. In retrospect we discern psychological conditions propitious to the release of revolutionary energies. But to most contemporaries, and especially to Irish conservatives, this was not apparent at the time. The period 1890 to 1910 was a kind of Indian summer for the old Ascendancy. For much of this period the Tories were in power in England, pledged 'to kill Home Rule by kindness'. To many, it seemed as if they were succeeding. Gladstone's second Home Rule Bill (1893) was the last valiant effort of a very old man; when it was rejected by the Lords, most Liberals felt their party had done all that could be expected of it. The Tory policy was one of redress of economic grievances, on the rather Marxist assumption that Irish nationalism would thereby become extinguished. By the Wyndham Act of 1903, most Irish tenants were enabled to buy

their holdings: the landlords received a generously calculated pur-
chase price from the state, and the tenants were to repay this by an-
nuities. It was a large and imaginative measure, which brought
important social benefits, but it did not achieve its political end.
Parnell had understood the situation better when he said he did not
fear that economic concessions would bring about a political
weakening: 'If the people wax fat,' he had said, 'then they will
kick.'

Yet they did not kick all at once. From an Ascendancy point of
view, not only did the horizon of the politics of the United Kingdom look bright, but in Ireland itself the fall of Parnell seemed to
have ended the time of troubles. Irish energies were going into
channels which seemed politically harmless: the Gaelic Athletic
Association (founded in 1885); the Gaelic League, founded by
Douglas Hyde (1860–1949) in 1893; the National Literary Society,
and the theatre which became the Abbey, founded by Yeats and
Lady Gregory in 1899. It is true that the Irish Republican Brotherhood, 'the Fenians', were interested in all these movements – as they
were in Arthur Griffith's self-reliance movement, Sinn Fein (' Ourselves') – and that all these movements were touched by an exalted
and romantic nationalism, which they in turn further exalted.
Yeats's *Cathleen ni Houlihan* (1902), with the leading part played by
Maud Gonne, became 'almost a sacrament' to the young nationalists
of the time. Yeats himself, on his deathbed, was troubled by the
question of his responsibility for the Rising of 1916:

> Did that play of mine send out
> Certain men the English shot?

Contemporaries were more disposed to laugh than to shiver. The
stories of Somerville and Ross and the verses of Percy French set the
tone for many: Ireland was delightful, but on no account to be taken

LADY GREGORY
SIGHING FOR NEW WORLDS TO KILTARTANISE.

Lady Gregory, co-founder of
the Abbey Theatre, gently
satirized as a pillar of the
Gaelic literary movement

Below: two scenes from the
first performance of Yeats's
Cathleen ni Houlihan

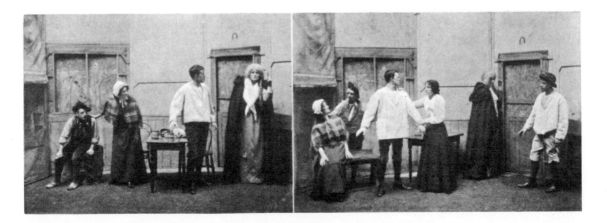

Royal visit to Dublin in 1900.
Dimly seen on the back seat is
the eighty-year-old Queen
Victoria

seriously. The young nationalists were harmless people – some of
them talented – engaged in the national pastime of play-acting, both
literally and metaphorically. Their specifically political activities –
their share in the rather confused and confusing centenary com-
memoration of 1798, and the attempted boycott of Queen Victoria's visit in 1900 – seemed more amusing than alarming. Yeats
himself became for a while 'certain' that he and his friends 'but
lived where motley was worn'.

They might, in retrospect, have come to be regarded as right in
this opinion, had not the political context of their lives become transformed through a shift in the balance between the main British
political parties, and a sharpening of class antagonisms in Britain.

The Tories, who were of course committed to resist Home Rule, went down in the Liberal landslide of 1906. Because it was a landslide, this did not have any great effect where Ireland was concerned: Campbell-Bannerman had a majority independent of the Irish representatives, and in these circumstances there was no need to take the risky – and to many Liberals repugnant – course of introducing a third Home Rule Bill.

After the general elections of 1910, however, the Liberals, with a seriously shrunken majority, became again dependent on the support of the Irish party: a Home Rule Bill was once more practical politics. This, in itself, need not have precipitated a grave crisis, if the Lords had still been in a position to kill such a Bill, as they killed that of 1892. But the Lords had undermined their own position by rejecting the Liberal budget of 1909; the Asquith government, with the conditional but real majority which it enjoyed after the two general elections of 1910, was now in a position to introduce a Parliament Bill, limiting the power of the Lords, and to carry this measure through the Lords by threatening to create new peers. Indeed, they were not merely in a position to do this: they were required to do it as the price of the Irish support on which their majority depended.

For the Irish party, now led by John Redmond, the opportunity seemed a heaven-sent one: the Parliament Act would open the door to Home Rule. The Irish could oblige the Liberals to introduce the Home Rule Bill, having previously deprived the Lords of the power to block it. Then the patient constitutional policy would be crowned with success, and the Sinn Fein and other extremists at home would be silenced by the solemn reopening of the Irish parliament in College Green.

Redmond and Home Rule

In purely parliamentary terms, all went for a while according to plan. The third Home Rule Bill – initially, like its two predecessors, intended to give limited self-government to Ireland as a unit – was introduced in April 1912 and had gone through all its stages in the Commons by January 1913. A fortnight later it was rejected by the Lords – as anticipated – and it was then carried once more through the Commons, and again rejected by the Lords in July 1913. In theory, granted the safe Home Rule majority in the Commons for the Bill, all that remained was to pass it again through the Commons, in which case rejection by the Lords could only delay its coming into operation; if pressed through in its original form it could have become law by the early summer of 1914.

Outside parliament, however, opposition to Home Rule developed formidable strength. The Ulster Protestants, for whom 'Home Rule' meant 'Rome Rule', were fundamentally opposed,

John Redmond, here seen
addressing a meeting in
Dublin in 1912, worked for
Home Rule by legal, parliamentary means

and they were a majority of the population in the industrialized
north-east. They were led by a gifted and determined Dublin Tory
lawyer, Edward Carson (1854–1935), whose object was if possible
to defeat Home Rule altogether (not just to keep Ulster out) and by
the British Tories, embittered by defeat in their successive general
elections, by the inroads into their stronghold in the Lords, by the
'social welfare' innovations of the post-Gladstonian Liberals, and
not least by the idea of Home Rule itself.

Ulster resistance   This opposition went to the length of threatening civil war, and
the threat was taken increasingly seriously. Drilling began in Ulster
early in 1912, and in January 1913 the Ulster Volunteer force was
officially formed. Very senior British officers on the retired list –
including Lord Roberts – took an openly benevolent interest in the
movement, and senior serving officers showed their sympathies more

discreetly, until in March 1914 it became known that fifty-seven officers of the Cavalry Brigade at the Curragh were prepared to resign rather than 'coerce Ulster'. King George V himself, showing alarm at the state of mind of the army, pressed the Prime Minister to exclude Ulster. It is hardly surprising that when, in April 1914, a large consignment of arms for the Ulster Volunteers was illegally landed at Larne, the police behaved like 'benevolent spectators'; and no action either then or later was taken against the law-breakers. The government, with Redmond's reluctant assent, now amended the Home Rule Bill, to allow Ulster counties to opt out, nominally for a period of six years, but in practice indefinitely. The Ulster Volunteers and their British political and military sympathizers, with some aid from royalty, had overborne the will of the elected representatives.

Edward Carson, Dublin Tory lawyer, fought for the exclusion of the Six Counties from Irish Home Rule, with the slogan 'Ulster will fight, and Ulster will be right'

Baton charge, 31 August 1913; crowds scattering before the police in O'Connell Street, Dublin

This was a period of bitter class struggle, both in England and in Ireland, and the recklessness of the Tory resistance to Home Rule was a part of this struggle. On the Irish side also, class militancy entered into the national struggle. From the great Dublin strike and lock-out of 1913 – about which Sean O'Casey later wrote his lyrical play, *Red Roses for Me* – there emerged James Connolly's Citizen Army, a working-class force which was also nationalist. Connolly's fusion of class militancy with revolutionary nationalism was later to win the approval of Lenin.

It was inevitable that the example of the Ulster Volunteers should be emulated – but towards a nationalist end – in the rest of Ireland. The British government could not prevent this development; it was hampered not only by its failure – or inability – to intervene in Ulster, but also by its dependence on Redmond's party. And Redmond came under increasingly heavy pressure in Ireland as the Liberals were forced to dilute their measure: partition was, of course, unacceptable to majority opinion in Ireland.

The Irish Republican Brotherhood, among whose council members were now the determined ex-convict Tom Clarke (1858–1916) and the poet Padraic Pearse (1879–1916), determined to take advantage of what it hoped might be a revolutionary conjuncture. The Irish Volunteers were founded in November 1913 under Redmond's nominal leadership, but strongly influenced by the IRB. At the end of July, guns for the Irish Volunteers were landed at Howth, Dublin: this time the forces of the Crown did try, belatedly, to interfere. Three civilians were killed.

The civil war towards which Ireland seemed to be drifting was averted, or postponed, by the outbreak of the First World War. Home Rule – with exclusion – was now on the statute book, but not to come into operation until the end of the war. Redmond and his colleagues supported the war effort and Irishmen volunteered in large numbers.

The Irish Republican Brotherhood, true to the traditional principle that England's difficulty was Ireland's opportunity, deter-

James Connolly and some of his Irish Citizen Army outside Liberty Hall, Dublin headquarters of the Irish Transport and General Workers Union, which Connolly founded

Many thousands of Irishmen, mostly followers of Redmond, joined the British Army – although their decisions were probably not much affected by posters like this

Sir Roger Casement

mined on armed insurrection at the earliest feasible date. As Redmond's followers left for service overseas, the Irish Volunteers who remained came increasingly under IRB influence. James Connolly (1870–1916), who had been openly calling for a rebellion, was taken – almost forcibly – into the counsels of the IRB. Help was sought from Germany, and many Volunteers considered such help to be an essential pre-condition for any insurrection. Germany, in the classic tradition of Ireland's continental allies, was interested in Ireland as an actual and potential source of embarrassment for England, but not interested enough to run serious risks in a remote and fairly well-guarded island. Roger Casement (1864–1916) returned to Ireland from an unsuccessful mission to Germany on 21 April 1916. His purpose was to inform the Volunteer leadership that no serious help would be forthcoming from Germany, and to call off the plans for a rising.

The IRB leaders, however, had made up their mind to strike a blow, irrespective of the chances of immediate success. They were influenced by the concept that previous insurrections, however unsuccessful, had kept the flame of nationality alive in the past, and by the fact that that flame seemed in early 1916 to be burning perilously low: about a hundred and fifty thousand Irishmen – all volunteers and mostly Catholics and nationalists following Redmond's lead – were then in British uniform, and recruiting was still going on. The IRB leaders thought that, however bad the chances might look in the spring of 1916, they would only get worse with the lapse of time. They set the date of the Rising for Easter Sunday, April 1916.

The Irish Volunteers enjoyed a measure of suspicious tolerance from the authorities mainly because of the embarrassing Ulster precedent, but also because both sets of Volunteers were officially though vaguely deemed – as the eighteenth-century Irish Volunteers had been deemed – to be a kind of militia which in this time of war would help to defend Ireland's shores from foreign invasion. This had been Redmond's concept, but those who now controlled the Volunteers considered that Ireland was already in the hands of a foreign invader, whose enemies were Ireland's allies. Dublin Castle knew that such ideas were at work but did not take them seriously – the 'manœuvres' set for Easter Monday were assumed to belong to the category of 'play-acting'.

The Commander-in-Chief of the Volunteers, Eoin MacNeill (1867–1945), a distinguished scholar and Gaelic Leaguer, was what would later have been called a 'front' for the real directorate, which was the IRB, of which MacNeill was not a member. He had not been included in the planning of the Rising and when he learned what was planned he issued an order countermanding the Easter

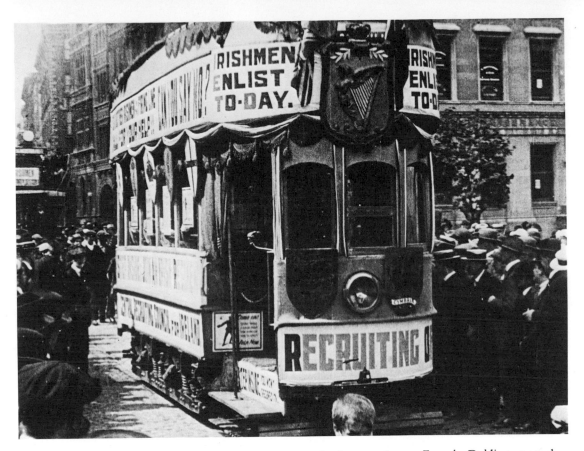

Even the Dublin trams took
part in the recruiting drive

Sunday manœuvres. 'Counter-countermanding orders' were then issued by the IRB officers.

As a result of this confusion, only about two thousand Volunteers out of the total of ten thousand – with about two hundred men of the Citizen Army – took part in the 'manœuvres' which became the Rising. The Rising, which had been intended to be nationwide, hardly spread beyond Dublin city. The rebels seized and held the General Post Office – which became the command post of Pearse and Connolly – and a number of public buildings and strategically situated premises. They proclaimed the Republic, which for the IRB leaders had long been 'virtually established'. The British forces were taken by surprise, and suffered fairly heavy casualties. Reinforcements arriving from England were held up by a small group of men firing from houses overlooking Mount Street Bridge: British casualties in this engagement were reported at 234 – almost half the total for the week of the Rising, on the British side. The Volunteer commandant in command in this sector was Eamon de Valera (b. 1882), later Prime Minister and afterwards President of Ireland.

The Easter Rising

POBLACHT NA H EIREANN.

THE PROVISIONAL GOVERNMENT
OF THE
IRISH REPUBLIC
TO THE PEOPLE OF IRELAND.

IRISHMEN AND IRISHWOMEN: In the name of God and of the dead generations from which she receives her old tradition of nationhood, Ireland, through us, summons her children to her flag and strikes for her freedom.

Having organised and trained her manhood through her secret revolutionary organisation, the Irish Republican Brotherhood, and through her open military organisations, the Irish Volunteers and the Irish Citizen Army, having patiently perfected her discipline, having resolutely waited for the right moment to reveal itself, she now seizes that moment, and, supported by her exiled children in America and by gallant allies in Europe, but relying in the first on her own strength, she strikes in full confidence of victory.

We declare the right of the people of Ireland to the ownership of Ireland, and to the unfettered control of Irish destinies, to be sovereign and indefeasible. The long usurpation of that right by a foreign people and government has not extinguished the right, nor can it ever be extinguished except by the destruction of the Irish people. In every generation the Irish people have asserted their right to national freedom and sovereignty; six times during the past three hundred years they have asserted it in arms. Standing on that fundamental right and again asserting it in arms in the face of the world, we hereby proclaim the Irish Republic as a Sovereign Independent State, and we pledge our lives and the lives of our comrades-in-arms to the cause of its freedom, of its welfare, and of its exaltation among the nations.

The Irish Republic is entitled to, and hereby claims, the allegiance of every Irishman and Irishwoman. The Republic guarantees religious and civil liberty, equal rights and equal opportunities to all its citizens, and declares its resolve to pursue the happiness and prosperity of the whole nation and of all its parts, cherishing all the children of the nation equally, and oblivious of the differences carefully fostered by an alien government, which have divided a minority from the majority in the past.

Until our arms have brought the opportune moment for the establishment of a permanent National Government, representative of the whole people of Ireland and elected by the suffrages of all her men and women, the Provisional Government, hereby constituted, will administer the civil and military affairs of the Republic in trust for the people.

We place the cause of the Irish Republic under the protection of the Most High God, Whose blessing we invoke upon our arms, and we pray that no one who serves that cause will dishonour it by cowardice, inhumanity, or rapine. In this supreme hour the Irish nation must, by its valour and discipline and by the readiness of its children to sacrifice themselves for the common good, prove itself worthy of the august destiny to which it is called.

Signed on Behalf of the Provisional Government,

THOMAS J. CLARKE,

SEAN Mac DIARMADA,   THOMAS MacDONAGH,
P. H. PEARSE,   EAMONN CEANNT,
JAMES CONNOLLY.   JOSEPH PLUNKETT.

Opposite: The proclamation of the Republic, Easter 1916. 'All the signatories were afterwards court-martialled and shot.' *Right:* a tattered Republican flag found by British troops in the house of a sympathizer, Countess Markievicz. during Easter week

Below: The Dublin General Post Office, headquarters of the Republican command, was a gutted shell by the time the Rising was defeated

Sir Roger Casement pleads 'Not Guilty' of treason. He had unsuccessfully sought German help for the Republican forces

After a week's fighting, and the shelling of the GPO, the rebels surrendered. Fifteen of the leaders, including Pearse, the wounded Connolly, and Clarke, were executed after court martial – and Casement was later tried and hanged.

All observers report that Dubliners, and Irish people generally, were at first almost unanimous in condemning the revolt; they also report that, after the executions, feeling very rapidly changed into one of veneration for the fallen leaders, and respect and support for their surviving comrades. From this it is sometimes inferred that if the British – specifically General Sir John Maxwell, responsible for punitive measures after the suppression of the Rising – had avoided the mistake of excessive harshness, all would have been well, in the sense that Ireland would have continued safely Red-mondite and would have peacefully evolved into a Canadian or Australian type of Commonwealth loyalty. The fact of the change of feeling is undoubted: it is also undoubted that it was at least greatly accelerated by revulsion against the executions. The extent and character of the change, however, suggest that there must have been a deep reserve of latent sympathy with the insurgents and of admiration for them; these forces would probably have found ex-pression in the aftermath of the crushing of the rebellion, even had the lives of the leaders been spared.

James Connolly

The Rising and its sequel destroyed the political base of the Irish parliamentary party led by Redmond. They too had been horrified at the number and protracted character of the executions, but their horror only underlined their helplessness. Popular support swung away from them, towards Sinn Fein. This was basically Griffith's organization, whose aim had originally been a dual monarchy, supposedly on Austro-Hungarian lines. Now it was to become the open political movement of the Republican revolutionaries. The British government probably underestimated the new movement; they were in any case obliged to be careful in their handling of it. Their Washington Embassy had reported the extremely adverse reaction of Irish-American – and some non-Irish American – opinion to the news of the 1916 executions. American reactions became a matter of acute concern to the British Government both before and shortly after America's entry into the war. A display of leniency became politically expedient, so several hundred interned insurgents, and some imprisoned ones, were released for Christmas 1916; more, including de Valera, were released in June 1917. De Valera immediately stood for election at a by-election in Clare, making the proclamation of 1916 his platform; he won by a large majority, and shortly afterwards was elected president of the re-organized Sinn Fein.

The first Dail Eireann, 1919.
Thirty-six elected members
were in jail

The British government's gesture of conciliation – including a
well-publicized but doomed effort to achieve all-Ireland and all-
party consensus through the Irish National Convention of 1917 –
became more perfunctory as time went on and America became
irrevocably committed to the war effort. Immediately after the Convention reported its failure, Lloyd George announced, on 9 April
1918, his intention to introduce legislation under which conscription could be applied to Ireland. Sinn Fein and the Irish party co-
operated in organizing protests and planning resistance against this,
but the nature of this campaign favoured the intransigence of Sinn
Fein, as against the party which had so long favoured co-operation
with a British government which, in wartime conditions, consistently disregarded its recommendations.

Conscription was never in fact imposed, though it remained a
threat up to the end of the war. The post-war general elections – in
December 1918 – brought the almost total elimination of the old
Irish party, which had monopolized the electoral representation of
Ireland – outside the Protestant north-east and Trinity College,
Dublin – for more than thirty years. The policy of Sinn Fein was to
refrain from taking the 73 seats (out of 105 for the whole of Ireland)

which it had won at Westminster, and to set up instead its own Republican parliament – Dail Eireann – open in principle to all elected representatives of Irish constituencies, but in practice a Sinn Fein assembly.

Dail Eireann – without 36 elected Sinn Fein members, who were in jail – met on 21 January 1919, ratified the Republic proclaimed in 1916, asserted the sole power of the Dail to make laws binding on the Irish people, and demanded 'the evacuation of our country by the English garrison'. By this, of course, was meant the evacuation of the whole island. The British government was now committed to partition; in substance this had been decided before the war, and the area to be excluded – the six counties which now constitute Nor, thern Ireland – had been determined during the war, at Carson's request. It represented the maximum area which the Protestant Unionists, in the opinion of their leaders, could securely hold. On

The first Dail

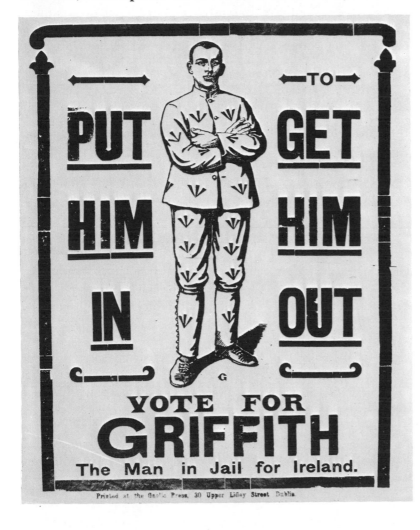

An effective election poster

this the British government was in no position to make concessions to Sinn Fein; it was also unprepared at this time to concede to the remaining twenty-six counties any significantly wider autonomy than what was contained in the Home Rule Bill of 1912. Dail Eireann and the British government were set on a collision course.

What form the collision would take was not immediately clear. Dail Eireann did not at once explicitly declare war on England. It is possible that many Sinn Feiners believed that their object could be obtained peacefully through the use of the boycott. Dail Eireann elected a government, of which the President was Eamon de Valera. It also set up its own Republican courts. Its authority, well based on popular support, was felt in varying degrees throughout Ireland, except in the Protestant north-east. Yet its authority over its own armed forces was uncertain. The Irish Republican Brotherhood, secret, oathbound and of its nature undemocratic, retained great influence. The Volunteer Executive accepted civilian control in theory, but not always in practice. And Volunteer officers in the field had sometimes a similar attitude towards the Volunteer command.

One of the declarations issued by Dail Eireann at its first meeting referred almost casually – as part of a long sentence – to 'the existing state of war, between Ireland and England'. This could be taken either metaphorically or literally. The literal construction was adopted almost immediately by the Volunteer Executive, which itself had been anticipated by armed action by a group of Volunteers, including Dan Breen, at Soloheadbeg, Co. Tipperary, on the day of Dail Eireann's first meeting.

The Troubles   There followed more than two and a half years of guerrilla war. The guerrillas – now known as the Irish Republican Army – had against them very heavy material odds. They probably never numbered more than about fifteen thousand men, armed with rifles, revolvers and shot-guns. The well-equipped British forces under General Macready numbered about forty-three thousand, with important para-military forces; the armed Royal Irish Constabulary, strengthened by recruits from England, selected for toughness – called 'Black-and-Tans' for their half-military half-police uniforms – and a force of ex-officers, organized as police auxiliaries.

The guerrillas had on their side the sympathy of the population into which they could merge before and after action. The 'fish' in Mao Tse-tung's terminology, did not lack 'water'. The British forces, inevitably, tried to break this sympathy by what is now called 'counter-terrorism': collective reprisals, carried out most conspicuously by Black-and-Tans and auxiliaries. The weakness of this was that it horrified many people in Britain – as well as in

Reconstruction of a typical incident in the guerrilla war of 1919–21, from a film made shortly afterwards

Canada and Australia – and many of Britain's supporters in Ireland, and was seriously damaging to Britain's relations with America. The guerrilla war, though bitter, was not more horrible than many other such struggles. What was exceptional about it was that it was conducted on a very brightly lit stage, and on what was regarded as home territory, and before an audience important to the Imperial power and containing an exceptional number of people either sympathetic to the guerrillas or revolted by the spectacle of what was necessary to repress them.

In these conditions the repression would have had to be conducted with exceptional efficiency and speed, in order to achieve political success. The IRA though very hard-pressed, held out long enough to make the work of repression a political burden to the British government. The sacrifice of the Lord Mayor of Cork, Terence

Death-mask of Terence
MacSwiney, Lord Mayor of
Cork

MacSwiney (1879–1920), who died after a hunger strike of seventy-
five days, became symbolic of Ireland's determination in resistance.
Irish risings in the past had been made to collapse with the aid of
informers. In this case, however, Michael Collins (1890–1922),
Director of Intelligence of the IRA and a guerrilla leader of genius,
not only eliminated informers on the Irish side, but successfully im-
planted his own informers in Dublin Castle, headquarters of the
repression. This factor, together with financial and moral support
from America – visited by President de Valera in 1919–20 – and
insurgent propaganda most ably conducted by Erskine Childers
(1870–1922), helped to make the military crushing of the rebellion
a protracted, costly and visible business and therefore politically un-
rewarding.

General elections were held in Ireland in May 1920. By this date
the 'home rule and partition' principles had become embodied in
the Government of Ireland Act, 1920, establishing separate parliaments for Northern Ireland and 'Southern Ireland'. The Unionists
had a solid majority in Northern Ireland. In 'Southern Ireland', the
Sinn Fein candidates were returned unopposed for every seat, except
for Trinity College. They refused, however, to take their seats in the
parliament of 'Southern Ireland' and continuing the previous procedure constituted the Second Dail.

The Government of Ireland Act was inoperative over most of Ireland, but it established a partition which has now endured for over half a century. Lloyd George's problem, which he set about with masterly political skill, was one of getting Dail Eireann, or at least a majority of its members, to accept the substance, though not necessarily the nomenclature, of the parliament of 'Southern Ireland'. Conditions were favourable for this. Most Irish people were sick of reprisals and counter-reprisals. They had voted for a Republic, and wanted an undivided one. Those of them who knew anything of Ulster, however, knew that no conceivable prolongation of guerrilla war in Republican Ireland could reunite Ireland. At the centre of the six counties of Northern Ireland was different 'water' supporting a different breed of 'fish'. And of course many ordinary Irishmen, who knew and cared little about Ulster, were ready to support any group which would accept a compromise capable of leading to peace.

On 25 June 1921, President de Valera received a letter from the Prime Minister of the United Kingdom, proposing a conference with a view to peace. A truce followed, on 9 July, and the discussions opened which were to lead to the Anglo-Irish Treaty. These negotiations, conducted in London, were complex and ambiguous and remain a subject of controversy; they cannot be adequately summarized. Essentially – though not in form – the main subjects of discussion consisted of Northern Ireland and 'Southern Ireland.' Could the Sinn Fein representatives – led by Griffith and Collins – 'recover' the six counties, or any form of authority over them, or even any part of the territory? And, in respect of 'Southern Ireland' –of which the British government recognized Sinn Fein as representative – what would be the extent of Sinn Fein's authority, and what its symbols: Crown or Republic?

From the British point of view, it was only the second set of questions that was under serious discussion, as is evident from the fact that Lloyd George's overture to de Valera was made immediately after the solemn opening of the parliament of Northern Ireland by the King. But Lloyd George, with immense subtlety and ingenuity, succeeded in convincing Griffith that Northern Ireland *might*, after all, in some way be brought in, provided the Sinn Fein representatives were reasonable on constitutional and defence issues. In this way the Irishmen were brought to accept – for the 'Southern Ireland' territory – an oath of allegiance to the Crown, control by Imperial forces of certain ports in peacetime and unlimited powers for the same forces in the time of war, 'or of strained relations with a Foreign Power'. The parliament of 'Southern Ireland' would become the parliament of the Irish Free State.

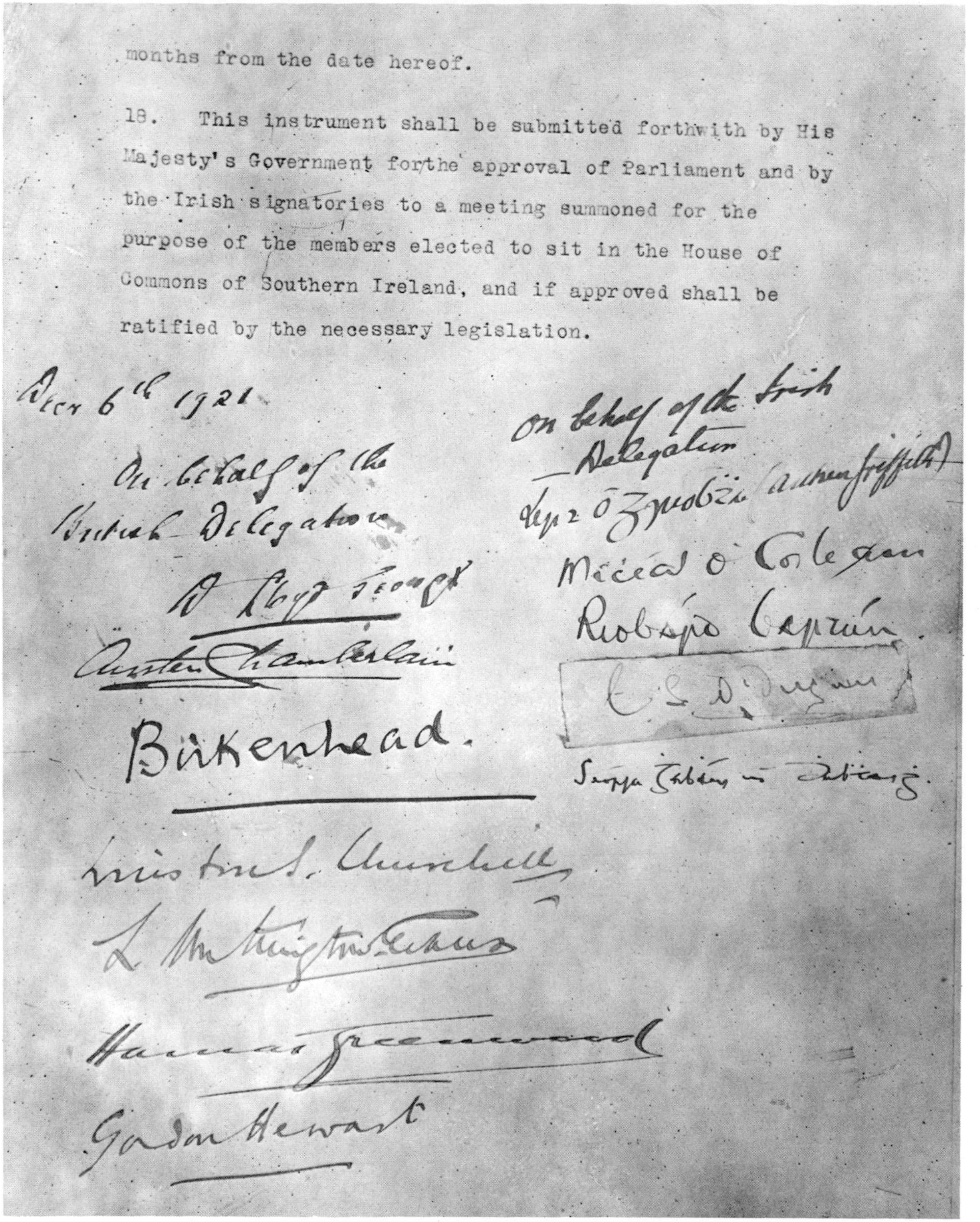

months from the date hereof.

18.   This instrument shall be submitted forthwith by His Majesty's Government for the approval of Parliament and by the Irish signatories to a meeting summoned for the purpose of the members elected to sit in the House of Commons of Southern Ireland, and if approved shall be ratified by the necessary legislation.

Decr 6ᵗʰ 1921

On behalf of the British Delegation

D Lloyd George

Austen Chamberlain

Birkenhead.

Winston S. Churchill

L. Worthington-Evans

Hamar Greenwood

Gordon Hewart

On behalf of the Irish Delegation

Art Ó Gríobhtha (Arthur Griffith)

Mícheál Ó Coileáin

Riobárd Bartún

E. S. Ó Dúgáin

Seorsa Gabháin uí Dhubhthaigh

Opposite: President de Valera (right) with Arthur Griffith whom he deputed to lead, with Michael Collins, the truce talks at 10 Downing Street. *Above:* The Treaty signed, December 1921. Neither side achieved all its demands

These arrangements resembled the substance of the British Go-vernment of Ireland Act much more closely than they did the absolute independence proclaimed by Sinn Fein. This was so even as far as 'Southern Ireland' was concerned. Northern Ireland was lost, and the apparent 'concessions' on it were totally illusory, since they depended on the agreement of the parliament of Northern Ire-land, which was the organized embodiment of refusal to make any such concessions.

Lloyd George's master-stroke was a Boundary Commission which could review the border between Northern and Southern Ireland. The Northerners understood – absolutely correctly as the event showed – that any revisions would in practice be quite mini-mal, and that the total territory of Northern Ireland would not be reduced. The Sinn Fein representatives, on the other hand, allowed themselves to be persuaded that the Boundary Commission's find-ings would result in the handing over to the Irish Free State of those large areas in Northern Ireland which had Catholic majorities, and that this loss of territory would in some way make the remainder of Northern Ireland unviable, thus bringing about the reunification of Ireland; this would be reward and justification for all the 'Southern' concessions. The remaining hesitations of the delegation were re-solved by a bravura performance by Lloyd George, threatening 'immediate and terrible war' if the Irish did not immediately sign. The Anglo-Irish Treaty was signed on 6 December 1921.

The Treaty   In most of Ireland most people received the news of the Treaty with immense relief. The main thing was that the British troops, and the hated Black-and-Tans and auxiliaries, would go home. About the terms of the Treaty, most people were uneasy but thought that they must have been the best that could be got and that if they were good enough for Michael Collins, no more need be said. In the IRA itself – for which the terms of the Treaty were far more un-palatable than they were for the population at large – many followed Collins, but many others, probably most, regarded the Treaty as treason to the Republic, and prepared to carry on the fight to the bitter end. De Valera sought revision of the terms of the Treaty – in relation especially to the important symbol of the oath of allegiance – in order to avert civil war. He was, however, defeated in the Cabi-net,.and – very narrowly – in the Dail (January 1922). The IRA split: separate forces, a Republican Army and a Free State Army, took shape and occupied different buildings in Dublin and else-where.

General elections (June 1922) produced a parliament with a safe pro-Treaty majority which elected a government headed by Arthur Griffith. There were Protestant pogroms against Catholics in

CHARGED WITH THE MURDER OF SIR HENRY WILSON: JOHN O'BRIEN.

SHOWING A BULLET-HOLE THROUGH THE DOOR: THE ENTRANCE TO SIR HENRY WILSON'S HOUSE, WHERE HE WAS MURDERED.

CHARGED WITH THE MURDER OF SIR HENRY WILSON: JAMES CONNOLLY.

Northern Ireland, and some military activity – supported for a time by both the pro-Treaty and anti-Treaty factions of Sinn Fein – against the Northern Ireland government, which called in as its adviser Sir Henry Wilson, former Chief of the Imperial General Staff, and an advocate of the reconquest of all Ireland. Wilson was assassinated by IRA men (22 June 1922). Lloyd George put pressure on the Griffith government to break definitely with the Republicans, if they wished to preserve the Treaty settlement. He also offered military assistance, which was eventually accepted. Early in the morning of 22 June, Free State forces, using field-guns borrowed from the British authorities, opened fire on the Four Courts, held by anti-Treaty forces. The Irish Civil War had begun.

The pro-Treaty forces were probably, in the beginning, numerically inferior, but they had the decisive advantages of superior material and supplies and also of the support of the great majority of the people. De Valera attached himself to the Republican side, but did not lead it: he seems to have favoured what would have been, in effect, a token resistance, proving that the Treaty settlement was accepted, by many Irishmen, only under duress. The Free State forces, by the end of the summer of 1922, held all the main cities, and most of the countryside. The Catholic hierarchy – which had given considerable moral support to Sinn Fein from 1918 on – condemned the anti-Treaty forces and placed them under excommunication. The struggle continued on guerrilla lines, and became more bitter after the killing of Michael Collins in an ambush at

Dunne and O'Sullivan, the assassins of Sir Henry Wilson, military adviser of the Northern Ireland government. At the time of their arrest they gave false names

151

Michael Collins, signatory of the Treaty and Commander-in-Chief of the Irish Free State Army (left), was ambushed and killed by his own countrymen in 1922

Bealnablath, Co. Cork (22 August 1922). The government began to apply ruthlessly a policy of reprisal executions, in which Erskine Childers and many others perished. Outside opinion could have little effect on this native government, and domestic opinion – however shocked at the executions – accepted the government as legitimate and wanted peace. This time the guerrilla fish had run out of water. They abandoned their resistance on 24 May 1923.

CHAPTER 8

Self-Government

The fighting of 1916, of 1918–21 and of the Civil War had produced in the end – old Redmondites would argue with some force
– no more than 'home-rule-without-Ulster' which could have been
obtained by Redmond's methods, without loss of life. Yet the Irish
Catholics in what is now the Republic never repudiated Sinn Fein
as they had repudiated Redmond: they continued – and continue
to this day – to support one or other of the factions into which Sinn
Fein broke. There was bitterness and disillusion in the wake of the
Civil War – as reflected for example indirectly in the plays of Sean
O'Casey, and directly in those of Denis Johnston – but there was
also pride: a common pride in what had been endured from 1916
to 1921, and two distinct proud traditions stemming from the Civil
War. The victors were proud of their realism, efficiency and responsibility and of the memory of their leaders, Griffith and Collins:
the vanquished, of their fidelity to the call of 1916, and the long new
roll of martyrs in that cause. Both traditions – but especially the
second – proved to have a remarkably enduring appeal.

Sean O'Casey: bitterness and
disillusion, but also a common
pride

The first government of the Irish Free State, under William T.
Cosgrave, had to set about a dual task. Domestically it had to provide conditions for the rebuilding of a badly damaged society and
economy. Inheriting a cautiously efficient civil service it set about
this task with energy, on conservative assumptions, and with a fair
measure of success. The Shannon hydro-electric scheme was useful
both in itself and as a visible symbol of peaceful construction in a
war-torn country. The second – and politically even more important – task was a constitutional one: that of proving that the Treaty
was not a betrayal of the national aspirations, but a gateway towards
their achievement. Here the Cosgrave government achieved much,
but not enough. It played a significant part in the development of

The Irish Free State

The Shannon hydro-electric scheme, a visible symbol of peaceful construction

the British Empire into a Commonwealth of sovereign nations. By 1931, the Irish Free State had achieved the substance of political sovereignty, although the defence provisions of the Treaty made it doubtful how real that sovereignty would remain in case of Britain's involvement in war. But the diplomatic and constitutional gains of the Cosgrave government were cancelled in the eyes of the electorate by what was regarded as a major national failure. In 1925, the government was obliged to recognize the existing border between the Free State and Northern Ireland: the Boundary Commission, in respect of which such extravagant hopes had been held out, yielded nothing at all. This seemed to many a powerful vindication of the anti-Treaty Cassandras, and therefore of Eamon de Valera.

De Valera had been imprisoned in 1923–24, as had many of his followers. Those of them who were elected members of the Dail refused to take their seats, because of the oath of allegiance required under the Treaty. In 1926, however, breaking with the intransigent Republicans, de Valera formed a new party, Fianna Fail ('Soldiers of Destiny'), which contested the elections of the following year; after these elections, he and members of his party took their seats in the Dail, having gone through a procedure which was accepted as complying with the requirements of the oath. In the same year Civil War passions were to some extent revived as the result of the murder of the Minister for Justice, Kevin O'Higgins (b. 1893), generally identified with the most ruthless, or determined, aspects of the government's policy. Measures of public security taken by the government in the wake of the O'Higgins murder aroused considerable opposition, and there was some armed activity conducted in the name of the IRA. In the general elections of 1932, bitterly fought but fairly conducted, Fianna Fail won a majority and Cosgrave and his colleagues handed over the seals of office to de Valera and his.

It was a notable example – perhaps unique in a newly independent state – of the victors in a civil war peacefully relinquishing office to representative figures among the losers in that war.

De Valera had to contend in the beginning with some paramilitary opposition, both from the Republican left, still claiming the IRA title, and from the Blueshirt movement on the right, which used some of the symbols and language of the contemporary Fascist movements. Both of these movements were, however, reduced to comparative insignificance by firm and skilful handling. The early years of the de Valera government were a period of economic difficulty both because of the general depression and because of the so-called 'economic war' with Britain resulting from de Valera's repudiation of the Land Annuity debt, and his early practice of unilaterally revoking provisions of the Anglo-Irish Treaty.

First stamp of the Irish Free State – overprinted on King George's head

Eamon de Valera, veteran of 1916, first President of the rebel Republic and
stubborn opponent of the Anglo-Irish Treaty, became Prime Minister (Chairman
of the Executive Council, later Taoiseach) in 1932. At the League of Nations (*opposite*)
he supported the policy of collective security, but when sanctions failed, he retreated
into neutrality. When war came, it was a policy of his government that Irish territory
should not be used as a base of operations against England

At the League of Nations, de Valera supported a policy of sanctions against Italy in the Abyssinian crisis. Although there was some opposition to this at home on grounds of sympathy with Catholic Italy, de Valera's stand on a principle – that of the interest of the smaller nations in the maintenance of collective security – was rather widely felt to have enhanced his stature. It also showed that, contrary to his reputation, his was not a policy of mere England-baiting, since the initiative he supported on this critical occasion was an English one. To him, however, the failure to implement sanctions during this crisis conveyed the lesson that collective security was, in the conditions of the 1930s, a mirage and that neutrality was the wisest policy for a small country.

Eire   It remained doubtful whether Ireland could be neutral if Britain was at war: defence provisions of the Treaty seemed to exclude this possibility. De Valera, however, succeeded in negotiating, with the Chamberlain government in 1938, a settlement which both ended the economic war and abrogated the defence provisos of the Treaty, giving Ireland full control over its own ports. The substantial sovereignty of the former Free State – now known as Ireland (Eire) under de Valera's Constitution of 1937 – was untrammelled. Partition, however, remained, as a legacy and symbol of past conquest. It was both a pretext for neutrality and a symptom of deeper, historical reasons for the support given by the great majority of Irishmen, outside Northern Ireland, to Irish neutrality, declared in September 1939.

There were those who held, in the tradition of Tone and of Pearse, that England's difficulty was Ireland's opportunity, and that aid should therefore be sought from, and given to, the Third Reich.

The huge revolving drum, crammed with hopeful counterfoils, is typical of the well-publicized gamblers' optimism that built the modern hospitals of Ireland

De Valera could hardly have contested the Republican orthodoxy of this argument, but he interned those who acted on it, or seemed likely to act on it. It was a cardinal principle of his wartime policy that Ireland's territory would not be allowed to serve as a base of operations against England. Confidence that he meant what he said and that his government, with overwhelming popular support, was in the best position to secure this result, were probably the principal reason – in addition to luck – why Irish neutrality was in fact respected.

The Irish state in the aftermath of the war felt its isolation, psychologically and intellectually. It had had for years a censorship of literature, aimed against obscenity but so interpreted as to attempt to exclude all modern imaginative prose writings of importance. This censorship law, together with laws against divorce and contraception, had been passed, under clerical pressure, in the period after the Civil War; these laws have never been repealed, although in prac-

One of the hospitals, built with money thus channelled: the Cherry Orchard Hospital, Ballyfermot, Dublin, built in 1953, has 280 beds

tice the censorship of literature has been greatly relaxed. To the censorship of literature had been added, during the war, a strict censorship of the press. With the ending of press censorship, Irish people found themselves strangers, and not very popular ones, in a strange post-war world.

De Valera, whose leadership had been accepted by almost all in the war period, now began to lose support. The young men whom he had interned (with general approbation at the time) now began to attract, by a familiar process, some retrospective and retroactive sympathy. The Clann na Poblachta party, founded and led by Sean MacBride – an attractive and dashing figure, son of one of the 1916 martyrs and of Maud Gonne, and former Chief of Staff of the IRA – won away some support from Fianna Fail. The de Valera government, after sixteen years continuously in office, fell in 1948 and was replaced by an inter-party government, whose components ranged from de Valera's right-wing opponents – the old Cosgrave party now known as Fine Gael – to the ultra-Republican left in Clann na Poblachta. This coalition was led by an eminent lawyer, John A. Costello.

Domestically the main achievements of the inter-party government were in the field of public health. The Fianna Fail government in the pre-war years had carried out a large programme of slum clearance, new housing and hospital construction (with the aid of the Irish Hospital Sweeps) but all such programmes had had to be suspended during the war. Ireland's public health statistics remained significantly worse than those of western Europe generally. The Minister for Health in the inter-party government, Dr Noel Browne, an associate of Sean MacBride's, attacked those problems vigorously – especially the eradication of tuberculosis – and won widespread esteem.

Leaving the Commonwealth Politically, the period of the inter-party government was marked by a renewed attempt to finish the unfinished business of the Treaty. As far as 'Southern Ireland' was concerned, this was now not difficult. The link with the Crown was finally severed by the Republic of Ireland (1949). Ireland (twenty-six counties) was now a Republic outside the Commonwealth. The Attlee government had no serious objection to what was essentially a symbolic change. The change was accompanied, however, on the Irish side, by rhetoric suggesting that a step had in some way been taken towards the ending of partition. The British government felt it advisable to reiterate in the Ireland Act (1949) that no such change would be made without the consent of the parliament of Northern Ireland. De Valera, on his fall from office, had gone on a world tour to present the case for the reunification of Ireland. The Ireland Act

was the signal for an all-party anti-partition campaign. This had no
visible effect either on international opinion or on partition. Its only
significant result was that Ireland became committed to the propo-
sition that it would not join NATO as long as partition remained.

In 1951 the inter-party government fell from office on an issue
which involved relations between Church and State. Dr Noel
Browne had prepared a far-reaching mother-and-child health
scheme. This aroused strong opposition from the medical profession, as representing the beginning of socialized medicine. Mr Costello thought it necessary to consult, and to announce that he had
consulted, the Catholic Archbishop of Dublin, who revealed that
a mother-and-child health scheme without a means test was contrary to the moral law. The government dropped the scheme,
Mr MacBride called for and obtained Dr Browne's resignation and
the government went to the country. The Clann na Poblachta party
was obliterated (though Dr Browne himself was re-elected) and
Mr de Valera returned to office. With the brief and relatively un-

Corpus Christi procession in
Killarney; the devout guard
are drawn from the Ambulance
Corps of the Knights of Malta

eventful exception of the second inter-party government (1955–57), de Valera's party has remained in office to the time of writing.

The fate of Dr Browne's scheme is usually invoked to show that politics in the Republic are dominated by the Church. The reality is not quite so simple as that: it was, after all, the government which showed such exemplary eagerness to be guided by the moral law (as expounded by the Archbishop) which was rejected by the electorate. What was really shown was that the Church is indeed a force in Irish politics, but one which it is dangerous to invoke.

From 1951 to 1969, Irish politics and Irish life generally, followed a fairly humdrum course. The retirement of Mr de Valera from

active politics and his election to the symbolic office of President (1959) was itself symbolic: the living link with the heroic politics of 1916 was now 'above politics'. The politics above which he is were sensible and mundane. His successor, Sean Lemass, openly abandoned the impossible and frustrating task of trying to end partition by diplomacy and propaganda, and attempted a good-neighbour policy with Northern Ireland. Decreasing emphasis was laid on the Irish language, the restoration of which was among the principal aims of Pearse and de Valera. Domestic politics turned increasingly on bread-and-butter issues. In foreign policy for some years, principally from 1957 to 1961, the Minister for External

Jack Lynch, Prime Minister of the Republic, addresses a Fianna Fail rally. The face on Mr Lynch's left is that of Mr Charles Haughey's, the Minister for Finance, whose dismissal by Mr Lynch, in May 1970, was one of many unforeseen consequences of events in Northern Ireland in April 1969

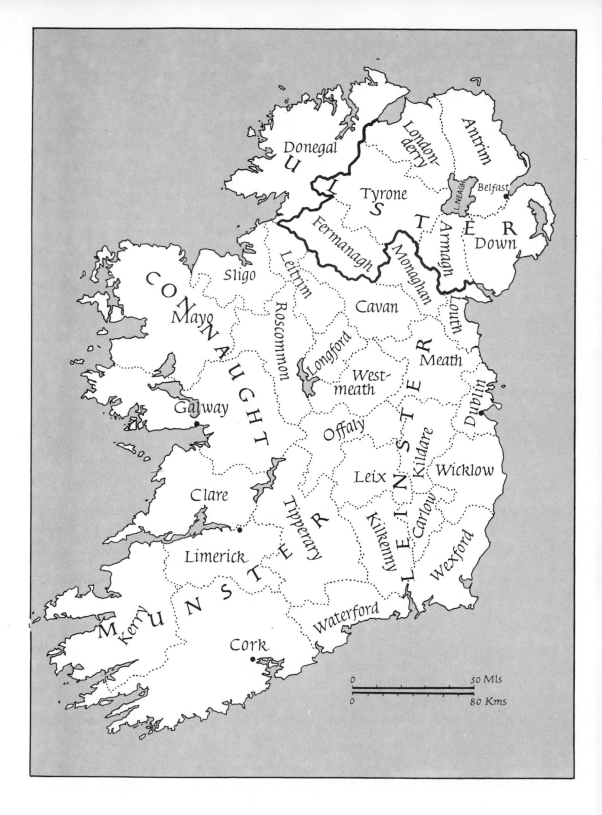

Affairs, Mr Frank Aiken, pursued an independent line at the United Nations, aimed at the reduction of cold-war tensions. The first move for the non-dissemination of nuclear weapons was made by Mr Aiken. As the decade wore on, however, the government's policy became more conventionally 'Western', and more congenial to the United States.

NORTHERN IRELAND

The six counties which the partition settlement placed under the control of the government of Northern Ireland seemed to evolve completely separately from the rest of the island. The last shadowy constitutional link between the two areas was broken when Ireland (twenty-six counties) left the Commonwealth in 1949, while Northern Ireland remained part of the United Kingdom.

Harland and Wolff's Belfast shipyard: the world's largest building dock floats a 250,000-ton tanker, the *Esso Ulidia*

Dublin's demands for the 'reunification' of Ireland sounded increasingly unreal and lacking in conviction. Yet it was around what this demand represented that the politics of Northern Ireland turned, in so far as they turned at all. The population of the Republic was almost homogeneous: that of Northern Ireland was not. In the Republic the very small minority of Protestants (5 per cent) accepted the institutions of the state and represented no political threat. In Northern Ireland, however, the Catholic minority (33 per cent)

Silent and grimly watchful: the Bogside, Londonderry's Catholic slum

did present a threat to a settlement which they were known to op-
pose. A substantial minority in the Six County unit, they were an
actual majority over wide territories, principally along the borders
with the Republic, with which they felt themselves in sympathy.

In these circumstances, and granted the past history of the area, it
is not surprising that Ulster Protestants, through whose armed
pressure Northern Ireland had come into existence, should regard the
Catholic population as a sort of fifth column, against which pre
cautions had to be taken. In so far as guerrilla activities were a threat
– as they were sporadically in every decade – it was the Catholic
population that constituted the 'water' for the 'fish': and the
border did not effectively divide the water. Guerrillas of the IRA
could count on sympathizers among the Catholic population on
both sides of the border.

Triumphing: a Protestant
procession in Ballymena

This situation had important political and social consequences. Politically, Protestant fears of a Catholic threat became the stock-in-trade of the Unionist Party. These fears have furnished that party with an unbroken monopoly of political power, through the support of almost the whole Protestant population, since the foundation of Northern Ireland. And this power, naturally, was used against those from fear of whom it derived: the Catholics. This use of power was unspectacular but effective. Key localities with Catholic majorities were gerrymandered to produce Protestant councils: these councils in turn gave jobs and houses to Protestants in preference to Catholics. In such ways, Catholics were encouraged to emigrate in numbers adequate to compensate for their higher birth-rate.

This system continued unshaken from 1920 to 1968. Dublin's occasional protests against it, combined with abstract demands for the end of partition, merely served to justify the system in the eyes of its architects. London, where the ultimate authority rested, showed no interest. No doubt the stability of the system was itself an argument in its favour: for much of the period, also, the fact that the Catholics could be seen as a threat to the security of a part of the United Kingdom would, as so often in the past, be thought of as justifying special measures in relation to them. A generation of Northern Catholics themselves became embittered, outnumbered in the North and effectively abandoned by the South, prisoners in a system created against them.

Two tribal symbols, typifying Ulster's tragic, historic enmities: *above*, Rev. Ian Paisley, M.P.; *opposite*, Miss Bernadette Devlin, M.P.

Nail bombs and barricades,
C.S. gas and rubber bullets,
rifles and gelignite – at the time
of writing, this chapter is not
yet closed. Protestant and
Catholic, North and South –
all have their fates involved
in it

Yet the generation of Northern Catholics born after the Second World War benefited, like the rest of the working class and unemployed throughout the United Kingdom, from the Welfare State. They were not discriminated against in terms of services or benefits controlled from London. This generation was better educated, more self-confident and less Dublin-oriented than earlier ones.

The Civil Rights movement

It was from this generation, and from some Protestants, mainly students and graduates of Queen's University, Belfast, that the Civil Rights movement derived its original strength in the late 1960s. This movement, in its initial phase, was non-violent, and concentrated on the objective of securing equal civil rights for all in Northern Ireland. As, in practice, those who had been deprived of these rights were Catholics, it was from Catholics exclusively that the movement – when it got going outside an educated urban milieu – derived its mass support. Correspondingly, it attracted people from the IRA and extreme left, interested in what they believed to be its revolutionary potential. Correspondingly also, it revived the fears of the Protestant majority, and therefore drew down the repression of the Protestant-controlled police, sometimes in collusion with crowds of Protestant activists.

This spectacle reached the British and world public through the television camera and evoked a wave of interest in, and sympathy with, the Civil Rights demonstrators unprecedented in the history of Northern Ireland. In August 1969, the Catholic quarter of Derry – the Bogside – resisted a police attempt to force an entry into it. As a result, serious sectarian fighting broke out in Belfast where – as Catholics there are outnumbered three to one – it mainly took the form of Protestant shooting at Catholics, and burning of Catholic houses. The British government then intervened, using the army, and placing the police under army control. The far-reaching repercussions of these events immediately began to affect the life, not only of Northern Ireland, but of the Republic also. Among the repercussions has been a revival of armed IRA activity and a wave of alarm among Protestants.

It is, as yet, far too early to attempt to write the chapter in Irish history which opened in August 1969. That chapter is not yet closed. At the time of writing, Catholics and Protestants seem as far as ever from being able to work out ways of existing peacefully together in the island which they share, and whose history they inherit. British government in the past did much to shape that history, and the British public of today, willy-nilly, inherits it. It may be that the beginning of wisdom in this matter – for Catholics as well as Protestants, English as well as Irish – is to see this history not as a repository or arsenal of grievances and titles to triumph, nor as something merely boring which may be tossed aside or shaken off, but as a common inheritance with multiple aspects. The hardest problem is to break the comfortable habit of seeing the inheritance in one accustomed set of aspects only, and to try to get used to the light in which the others who also inherit it are accustomed to seeing it. This book has no pretensions to solving that problem: all it claims is to try to make somewhat more widely known some of the results of the work of those historians of Ireland, many of them recent, who have written not to validate competing myths but to find a common historical language in which we today can communicate, with a minimum of recrimination, complacency or boasting, about a past which has moulded us, and also threatens us.

The Border

Bagwell, Richard, *Ireland under the Tudors*. London, 1885–90
   Ireland under the Stuarts. London, 1909–16
Binchy, D. A. (ed.), *Studies in Early Irish Law*. Dublin, 1936
Brown, T. N., *Irish and American Nationalism, 1870–1890*. Philadelphia and New
   York, 1966
Carney, J., *The Irish Bardic Poet*. Dublin, 1967
Case, Humphry, and Arthur ap Simon, *The Neolithic and Earlier Bronze Ages in the
   North of Ireland*. Belfast, 1970
Chubb, Basil, *The Government and Politics of Ireland*. London and Stanford, Calif.,
   1970
Clarke, A., *The Old English in Ireland, 1625–42*. London, 1966
Cornell, Kenneth, *The Population of Ireland, 1750–1845*. Oxford, 1950
Connolly, James, *Labour and Easter Week*. Dublin, 1949
   The Workers' Republic. Dublin, 1951
Coogan, Timothy P., *Ireland since the Rising*. London and New York, 1966
   The I.R.A. London, 1970
Corkery, Daniel, *The Hidden Ireland: a study of Gaelic Munster in the eighteenth century*.
   Dublin, 1925
Curtis, Edmund, *A History of Medieval Ireland: 1086–1513*. London, 1938
de Paor, Máire and Liam, *Early Christian Ireland*. London, 1958
de Vere White, Terence, *Kevin O Higgins*. London, 1948
Dillon, Myles, and Nora Chadwick, *The Celtic Realms*. London, 1967
Edwards, R. Dudley, *Church and State in Tudor Ireland*. Dublin, 1935
Edwards, R. Dudley, and T. D. Williams (eds), *The Great Famine*. Dublin, 1956
Evans, Estyn, *Prehistoric and Early Christian Ireland, a guide*. London, 1966
Falls, Cyril, *Elizabeth's Irish Wars*. London, 1950
FitzGerald, Brian, *The Geraldines, an Experiment in Irish Government, 1169–1601*.
   London, 1951
Froude, J. A., *The English in Ireland in the Eighteenth Century* (5 vols). London, 1892
Greaves, C. D., *The Life and Times of James Connolly*. London, 1961
Greene, David W., *The Irish Language*. Dublin, 1966
Hammond, J. L., *Gladstone and the Irish Nation*. London and Hamden, Conn., 1964
Hanson, R. P. C., *Saint Patrick, his origins and career*. Oxford, 1968
Henry, Françoise, *Irish Art in the Early Christian Period to AD 800*. London, 1965
   Irish Art during the Viking Invasions, 800–1020. London, 1967
   Irish Art in the Romanesque Period, 1020–1170. London, 1970

Hughes, Kathleen, *The Church in Early Irish Society*. Cambridge, 1966

Inglis, Brian, *The Freedom of the Press in Ireland, 1784–1841*. London, 1954

Kenny, J.F., *Sources for the Early History of Ireland: ecclesiastical*. New York, 1929

Knott, Eleanor, and Gerard Murphy, *Early Irish Literature*. London, 1966

Larkin, Emmet, *James Larkin, Irish Labour Leader, 1876–1947*. London, 1965

Lecky, W.E.H., *History of Ireland in the Eighteenth Century* (3 vols, 2nd ed.). London, 1881

Lyons, F.S.L., *The Irish Parliamentary Party, 1890–1910*. London, 1951
    The Fall of Parnell, 1890–91. London, 1960

Macardle, Dorothy, *The Irish Republic* (4th ed.). Dublin, 1951; New York, 1965

MacCarra, Proinsias, *Celtic Mythology*. London, 1970

MacCurtain, Margaret (ed.), *A History of Ireland*. Dublin, 1969

MacDermot, Frank, *Theobald Wolfe Tone*. London, 1939

MacDowell, R.B., *Irish Public Opinion, 1750–1800*. London, 1944
    Public Opinion and Government Policy in Ireland 1801–1846. London, 1952

MacIntyre, Angus, *The Liberator: Daniel O'Connell and the Irish party, 1830–1847*. London, 1965

MacLysaght, Edward, *Irish Life in the Seventeenth Century: after Cromwell* (2nd ed.). Cork, 1950

Mansergh, Nicholas, *The Irish Question, 1840–1921* (new ed.). London, 1965

Moody, T.W., *The Londonderry Plantation*. Belfast, 1939

Moody, T.W., and J.C. Beckett (eds), *Ulster since 1800*, 2 series: (i) *A Political and Economic Survey*, London, 1955; (ii) *A Social Survey*, London, 1957

Moody, T.W., and F.X. Martin (eds), *The Course of Irish History*. Cork, 1967. (This valuable collection of essays from several hands covers the same span as the present work.)

Nowlan, Kevin, *The Politics of Repeal: a study in the relations between Great Britain and Ireland, 1841–50*. London and Toronto, 1965

O'Brien, Conor Cruise, *Parnell and His Party, 1880–90*. Oxford, 1957; corrected impression, 1964
    (ed.) *The Shaping of Modern Ireland*. London, 1960; reprinted 1970

Ó Broin, Leon, *Dublin Castle and the 1916 Rising*. Dublin, 1966

O'Connell, Maurice R., *Irish Politics and Social Conflict in the Age of the American Revolution*. Philadelphia, 1965

Ó Cuív, Brian (ed.), *Seven Centuries of Irish Learning, 1000–1700*. Dublin, 1961
    A View of the Irish language. Dublin, 1969

Ó Faoláin, Séan, *King of the Beggars* (a life of Daniel O'Connell). London, 1938
    The Great O Neill. London, 1943

O'Hegarty, P.S., *A History of Ireland under the Union, 1801 to 1922*. London, 1952

O Kelly, Claire, *Illustrated Guide to New Grange*. Wexford, 1967

O Neill, Thomas P., and the Earl of Longford, *Eamon de Valera*. London, 1970

O'Rahilly, T.F., *Early Irish History and Mythology*. Dublin, 1946

Ó Riordáin, S.P., *Antiquities of the Irish Countryside*. London, 1964

Ó Riordáin, S.P., and Glyn Daniel, *New Grange and the Bend of Boyne*. London, 1964

Orpen, G.H., *Ireland under the Normans, 1169–1333*. 4 vols. Oxford, 1911–20

Otway-Ruthven, A.J., *A History of Medieval Ireland*. London and New York, 1968

Pakenham, Frank, *Peace by Ordeal*. London, 1935; new ed., 1962

Pakenham, Thomas, *The Year of Liberty: the story of the Great Irish Rebellion of 1798*. London, 1969

Powell, T.G.E., *The Celts*. London, 1963

Quinn, D.B., *The Elizabethans and the Irish*. Ithaca, New York, 1966

Raftery, Joseph, *Prehistoric Ireland*. London, 1951

(ed.) *The Celts*. Cork, 1967

Ryan, Desmond, *The Fenian Chief: a biography of James Stephens*. Dublin, 1967

Schrier, Arnold, *Ireland and the American Emigration, 1850–1900*. Minneapolis, 1958

Stewart, A. T. Q., *The Ulster Crisis*. London, 1969

Thornley, D. A., *Isaac Butt and Home Rule*. London, 1964

Wall, Maureen, *The Penal Laws, 1691–1760*. Dundalk, 1961

Watt, J. A., *The Church and the Two Nations in Medieval Ireland*. Cambridge, 1970

Williams, T. D. (ed.), *The Irish Struggle (1916–26)*. London and Toronto, 1966

Woodham-Smith, Cecil, *The Great Hunger*. London, 1962

The authors wish to thank in particular Dr F. S. L. Lyons and Dr G. A. Hayes-McCoy for much kind advice and criticism

19 The promontory fort of Dun-beg, Dingle peninsula, Co. Kerry. *Photo Edwin Smith.*

20 The hill-fort, Grianán of Ailech, Co. Donegal. *Photo Edwin Smith.*

21 Enamelled bronze horsebit, Early Iron Age, from Killevan, Co. Monaghan, *c.* 1st century AD. National Museum of Ire-land, Dublin.

Red enamelled bronze fibula, Early Iron Age, from Co. Galway, *c.* 3rd century BC. National Museum of Ireland, Dublin.

22 Ornamental disk on the bell-end of the Loughnashade horn. National Museum of Ireland, Dublin.

24 Shrine of St Patrick's Bell, *c.* 1091. Gold, bronze, silver. National Museum of Ireland, Dublin.

26 Ogham stone, Aglish, Co. Kerry. National Museum of Ireland, Dublin.

28 St Columba. Pen drawing from Adamnán's *Vita Sancti Colum-bae,* 9th century. MS 555, folio 166. Stiftsbibliothek, St Gallen, Switzerland.

29 Page from the Cathach of St Columba, folio 19r. Royal Irish Academy, Dublin. *Photo Green Studio, Dublin.*

30 Skellig Michael, Co. Kerry. Detail of the main enclosure. *Photo Commissioners of Public Works in Ireland.*

31 Doorway of Iona Cathedral, Hebrides. *Photo Edwin Smith.*

Celtic monastery on the island of Devenish in Lough Erne, Co. Fermanagh, founded 6th century. *Photo J. K. St Joseph; Crown copyright reserved.*

33 The Oseberg ship (restored). Universitetets Oldsaksamling, Oslo.

34 Figures on the Breac Maodhóg shrine, dating from the 11th century. National Museum of Ireland, Dublin.

The Ardagh Chalice from Ardagh, Co. Limerick. National Museum of Ireland, Dublin.

35 Chi-Rho page from the Book of Kells, folio 34r. Trinity College, Dublin.

36 The Round Tower, the island of Devenish, Lough Erne, Co. Fermanagh. *Photo Edwin Smith.*

37 The Cross of the Scriptures, Clonmacnoise. *Photo Irish Tour-ist Board.*

38 The imaginary ground-plan of the great banquet hall of the legendary High Kings of Tara, 12th century. From the Book of Leinster. By courtesy of the Board of Trinity College, Dublin.

39 Hiberno-Danish coin. Copy of a penny of Ethelred II struck in Dublin. Obverse. British Museum, London. *Photo Peter Clayton.*

40 Cormac's Chapel, Cashel, Co. Tipperary, consecrated 1134. *Photo Courtauld Institute of Art.*

42 Irish foot-soldier, from the time of Edward I. Chapter House, Liber A. *Photo Public Record Office, London.*

Strongbow's tomb in Christ-church Cathedral, Dublin. *Photo Irish Tourist Board.*

43 'King John's castle', Carling-ford, Co. Louth. *Photo Com-missioners of Public Works in Ireland.*

44 An Irish banquet. Scene from John Derrick's *Image of Ireland*, 1581. *Photo Mansell Collection.*

Irish monk, from *The Fauna of Ireland as described by Gerald of Wales*, MS Roy. 13 B viii, folio 22, 13th century. British Museum, London.

45 King Richard II's army in Ireland. From Richard II's Campaigns in Ireland, MS Harl. 1319, folio 7b. British Museum, London.

Art Mac Murrough Kavanagh meeting the Earl of Gloucester, King Richard II's envoy. From Richard II's Campaigns in Ireland, MS Harl. 1319, folio 9. British Museum, London.

Richard II crossing from Ireland to England. From Richard II's Campaigns in Ireland, MS Harl. 1319, folio 18. British Museum, London.

46 Portrait of King Edward III from the Waterford charter roll, executed late 14th century. Waterford Borough Council. *Photo Green Studio, Dublin.*

49 Irish noblewoman, possibly the first Countess of Ormond, 14th-century effigy, from the ruined part of St Mary's Church, Gowran, Co. Kilkenny. *Photo Commissioners of Public Works in Ireland.*

50 De Bermingham Castle at Athenry, Co. Galway, *c.* 1250. *Photo Commissioners of Public Works in Ireland.*

51 Rosserk Abbey, Co. Mayo, friary of Franciscan tertiaries founded in 1441. *Photo Camera Press.*

Fore Abbey, Co. Westmeath. *Photo Commissioners of Public Works in Ireland.*

52 Irish harp, traditionally believed to have belonged to King Brian Boru. By courtesy of the Board of Trinity College, Dublin. *Photo Green Studio, Dublin.*

53 Portrait of Edmund Spenser. By courtesy of the Master and Fellows of Pembroke College, Cambridge.

54 Submission of Turlough O'Neill to Sir Henry Sidney. From John Derrick's *Image of Ireland*, 1581. British Museum, London.

55 An Irish piper. From the *Ordinale of Rosglas*, early 16th century. MS Rawl. C. 32, folio 31v. Bodleian Library, Oxford.

An abbot. From the *Ordinale of Rosglas*, early 16th century. MS Rawl. C. 32, folio 54v. Bodleian Library, Oxford.

57 Title-page of the proclamation of Queen Elizabeth I to Ireland, 1576. By courtesy of the Board of Trinity College, Dublin. *Photo Green Studio, Dublin.*

58 Irish men and women, from the time of Elizabeth I. From *Corte beschryvinghe van England, Scotland, ende Irland*. Dutch, MS Add. 28330. British Museum, London.

59 Capture of Thomas, Earl of Ormond, Lieutenant-General of Queen Elizabeth's army in Ireland, by O'More, 10 April 1600. MS 1209 no. 13. By courtesy of the Board of Trinity College, Dublin. *Photo Green Studio, Dublin.*

60 The army of the King of Spain, commanded by Don Juan de Aguila at the siege of Kinsale, 17 October 1601. From Sir Thomas Stafford's *Pacata Hibernia*, 1633. National Library of Ireland, Dublin.

62 The plantation of Ulster: proposed fortification at Londonderry. Illustration from *A Survey of Irish Plantation* by Sir Thomas Phillips, 1662. *Photo Mansell Collection.*

Oliver Plunkett, Archbishop of Armagh. Painting by G. Murphy. National Gallery of Ireland, Dublin.

63 Jigginstown House, Co. Kildare. *Photo Irish Tourist Board.*

64–5 Scottish mercenaries in the service of Gustavus Adolphus, 1631. From a contemporary German broadsheet. British Museum, London. *Photo Mansell Collection.*

66 An Inchiquin crown, Charles I 'necessity money', coined in Ireland, 1642. British Museum, London. *Photo Peter Clayton.*

67 Petition of English soldiers in Ireland. From a broadsheet of 1648, folio 18. British Museum, London. *Photo Fleming.*

69 Sir Neill O'Neill. Painting by J.M. Wright, 1679. Tate Gallery, London.

70 Dublin coopers' charter, 1666. Guinness Museum, Dublin.

71 James, 1st Duke of Ormond. Portrait by Edmund Ashfield. National Gallery of Ireland, Dublin.

The Royal Hospital, Kilmainham, Dublin. Designed by Sir William Robinson, 1679. *Photo Camera Press.*

72 'Lilliburlero'. *Photo Mansell Collection.*

Satirical playing-card, showing Tyrconnell arming the Catholics. British Museum, London. *Photo Eileen Tweedy.*

73 Richard Talbot, Earl of Tyrconnell, 1690. Painting of the French School. National Portrait Gallery, London.

Broadsheet showing *Undaunted Londonderry*. British Museum, London. *Photo Mansell Collection.*

74 The Battle of the Boyne. Painting by Jan Wyck. National Gallery of Ireland, Dublin.

The flight of James II. His embarkation at Waterford, 12 July 1690. National Library of Ireland, Dublin.

74–5 A prospect of Limerick, 1691. British Museum, London. *Photo Mansell Collection.*

76 Suppression of the rebellion in Ireland, 1691. Medal showing Hercules killing the hydra, by Jan Luder. British Museum, London. *Photo Peter Clayton.*

77 A 'penal cross', Galway, 1712. National Museum of Ireland, Dublin.

78 Edmund Burke. Statue at Trinity College, Dublin. By courtesy of the Board of Trinity College, Dublin. *Photo Green Studio, Dublin.*

79 Portrait group showing George Berkeley, Protestant Bishop of Cloyne, with his wife and friends. Painting by John Smibert. National Gallery of Ireland, Dublin.

80 Jonathan Swift. Portrait by Francis Bindon. National Gallery of Ireland, Dublin.

81 Frontispiece and title-page from James Hardiman's *Irish Minstrelsy*, vol. 1, 1831. *Photo Eileen Tweedy.*

82 The Archbishop Cobbe anti-Pretender mammoth loving cup, *c.* 1745. Williamite glass. Ulster Museum, Belfast.

83 Silver-gilt mace of the old Irish House of Lords, made in Dublin, *c.* 1766. National Museum of Ireland, Dublin.

84 Henry Grattan. Portrait study by Francis Wheatley, 1782. National Portrait Gallery, London.

85 The Irish House of Commons. Painting by Francis Wheatley. Leeds City Art Galleries.

86 Silver medal of the 1st Ulster regiment of the Irish Volunteers, 1787. Ulster Museum, Belfast.

86-7 The Volunteers in College Green. Painting by Francis Wheatley. National Gallery of Ireland, Dublin.

88 View of the Four Courts, Dublin. Print by James Malton, 1799. National Library of Ireland, Dublin.

Custom House, Dublin. Print by James Malton, 1792. National Library of Ireland.

89 Theobald Wolfe Tone. Drawing from the Joly Collection. National Library of Ireland, Dublin.

Irish gratitude. Gillray cartoon on the proposed grant of money to Grattan, 13 June 1782. British Museum, London. *Photo Eileen Tweedy.*

90 The arrest of Lord Edward Fitzgerald, May 1798. Cartoon by George Cruikshank. *Photo Mansell Collection.*

The badge of the United Irishmen, taken from Lord Edward Fitzgerald, 19 May 1798. National Museum of Ireland.

91 The French in Killala Bay. Painting by William Sadler. National Gallery of Ireland.

92 Rebels destroying a house and furniture. Cartoon by George Cruikshank. *Photo Mansell Collection.*

93 Detail from *View of Westport House.* Painting by George Moore, 1760. Collection the Earl of Altamont. *Photo Irish Tourist Board.*

94-5 The Union Club. Cartoon by Gillray. *Photo Mansell Collection.*

96 The execution of Robert Emmet, 1803. National Library of Ireland.

97 Robert Emmet. Detail from a miniature by John Comerford. National Gallery of Ireland, Dublin.

98-9 Front view of Trinity College, Dublin. Watercolour by James Malton. National Gallery of Ireland, Dublin.

100 Daniel O'Connell and the Catholic Rent. Cartoon from *Punch,* 1842. *Photo Mansell Collection.*

101 Letter from Daniel O'Connell to William Cobbett, 20 November 1834. Add. MS 31022, folio 30. British Museum, London.

102 Portrait of Thomas Davis. Drawing by Frederick William Burton. National Gallery of Ireland, Dublin.

103 Flax drawing. From *The Pictorial Gallery of the Arts, c.* 1860. *Photo Radio Times Hulton Picture Library.*

104 *Outward Bound,* the quay of Dublin. Lithograph by T.H. Maguire after the painting by J. Nichol, 1854. Old Print Shop, New York.

The Battery, New York, c. 1855, showing Castle Garden as an immigration station. Panoramic painting by Samuel B. Waugh. Museum of the City of New York.

105 Potato famine in Ireland, 1846. Starving peasants at the gate of a workhouse. Engraving. *Photo Mansell Collection.*

107 St Patrick's Day parade in Union Square, New York, early 1870s. Coloured lithograph. The J. Clarence Davies Collection. Museum of the City of New York.

108 Interior of Mountjoy Prison, Dublin, where the Fenians were confined, 23 June 1866. *Photo Radio Times Hulton Picture Library.*

109 Michael Davitt in the new committee room of the Land League in Dublin. From *The Graphic*, 1881. *Photo Radio Times Hulton Picture Library.*

111 Eviction scene. National Library of Ireland, Dublin.

A tenant before the magistrate. From *The Graphic*, 1880. *Photo Radio Times Hulton Picture Library.*

The Land Agitation in Ireland. From *The Graphic*, January 1881. *Photo Mansell Collection.*

112 Portrait of Charles Stewart Parnell. Drawing by J. D. Reigh, 1891. National Gallery of Ireland, Dublin.

113 Kilmainham Jail. Interior view. *Photo Mansell Collection.*

114 The murder of Lord Frederick Cavendish and Mr Burke in Phoenix Park, Dublin. *Photo Radio Times Hulton Picture Library.*

115 Parnell represented as a national hero, before Balfour. From *United Ireland*, 1889. British Museum, London. *Photo Freeman.*

116 Balfour, Chief Secretary for Ireland, and the Coercion Act. Cartoon by F. Carruthers Gould, 1888, from the *Pall Mall Gazette.*

117 Britannia between Gladstone and Salisbury. Cartoon by J. D. Reigh. British Museum, London. *Photo Eileen Tweedy.*

118 Katharine O'Shea. *Photo Radio Times Hulton Picture Library.*

119 Parnell and Healy, depicted as the two villains of the Babes in the Wood. Cartoon by Tenniel from *Punch*, 20 December 1890. *Photo Mansell Collection.*

120–1 The port of Dublin in the 1880s. Guinness Museum, Dublin.

122 James Joyce, 1935. Painting by Jacques-Emile Blanche. National Portrait Gallery, London.

W. B. Yeats in 1907. Etching by Augustus John, 1907. National Portrait Gallery, London.

J. M. Synge, 31 December 1895. *Photo courtesy Lily M. Stephens.*

124 St Patrick's Royal College, Maynooth. *Photo Adolf Morath.*

126 Page from *Slipper's ABC of Foxhunting* by E. Œ. Somerville, 1903. British Museum, London. *Photo Fleming.*

127 Cartoon on Gladstone and the Home Rule Bill. From *Punch*, 15 April 1893. *Photo Fleming.*

128 Portrait group, showing Lord Ashbourne, President, and other leaders of the Gaelic League. National Gallery of Ireland, Dublin.

129 Lady Gregory sighing for new worlds to Kiltartanize. Cartoon by Grace Plunkett from *To hold as 'twere*, 1920. British Museum, London. *Photo Fleming.*

Scenes from *Cathleen ni Houlihan* by W. B. Yeats. Performance in 1902, in which Maud Gonne played the title-role. From *The Tatler*, 16 April 1902. *Photo Mander and Mitchenson Theatre Collection.*

130 Queen Victoria in her carriage during her visit to Dublin in 1900. Courtesy Robert C. Booth. Guinness Museum, Dublin.

132 Redmond addressing a meeting at the Parnell monument, Dublin, 1912. *Photo Independent Newspapers Ltd, Dublin.*

133 Sir Edward Carson addressing an anti-Home Rule meeting, September 1913. *Photo Radio Times Hulton Picture Library.*

134 Baton charge in O'Connell Street, 31 August 1913, during the great Dublin strike and lockout. *Photo Irish Transport and General Workers' Union, Dublin.*

135 Liberty Hall, Dublin, Headquarters of the Irish Transport and General Workers' Union, showing James Connolly and other members of the Irish Citizen Army. National Library of Ireland, Dublin.

136 Recruiting poster for the First World War. Imperial War Museum, London.

Sir Roger Casement, 1919. *Photo Radio Times Hulton Picture Library.*

137 Recruiting tram in Dublin, from the First World War. Courtesy Radio Telefis Eireann. *Photo James G. Maguire Studios.*

138 Proclamation of the Republic, Easter 1916. *Photo Irish Embassy, London.*

139 Republican banner taken after Easter Week, 1916, probably by the 3rd Battalion, Royal Irish Rifles. Now in the Irish National Museum, Dublin.

The Dublin General Post Office, where the Sinn Fein rebels made their most determined stand, and which they fired on 28 April 1916. *Photo Mansell Collection.*

140 Sir Roger Casement pleading not guilty from the dock, 1916. *Photo Mansell Collection.*

141 James Connolly. National Museum of Ireland, Dublin.

142 The first Dail Eireann, 1919. *Photo Lafayette.*

143 Election poster of Arthur Griffith. Imperial War Museum, London.

145 A Black-and-Tan search: still from film *The Dawn*. *Photo Radio Times Hulton Picture Library.*

146 Death-mask of Terence Mac-Swiney by Albert Power. National Museum of Ireland, Dublin.

148 De Valera and Griffith at the Irish Peace Conference, July 1921. *Photo Radio Times Hulton Picture Library.*

149 Signatures on the Irish Peace treaty, 6 December 1921. *Photo Radio Times Hulton Picture Library.*

151 Dunne and O'Sullivan, charged with the Wilson murder, 22 June 1922. *Photo Illustrated London News and Sketch Ltd.*